HOW TO DOWNLOAD THE WALKING EYE APP

Available on purchase of this guide only.
1. Visit our website: www.insightguides.com/walkingeye
2. Download the Walking Eye container app to your smartphone (this will give you access to your free eBook and the ability to purchase other products)
3. Select the scanning module in the Walking Eye container app
4. Scan the QR Code on this page – you will be asked to enter a verification word from the book as proof of purchase
5. Download your free eBook* for travel information on the go

* Other destination apps and eBooks are available for purchase separately or are free with the purchase of the Insight Guide book

TOP 10 ATTRACTIONS

CASA ROMANA
Zoological floor mosaics and other late-Roman treasures. See page 34.

CLIMBING HRISTÓS PEAK
For the Dodecanese's best views. See page 58.

WINDSURFING
Breezy Kos has several suitable shorelines. See page 85.

BROS THERMÁ HOT SPRINGS
Seaside magic by moonlight. See page 42.

KOS
POCKET GUIDE

◉ Walking Eye App

Your Insight Pocket Guide purchase includes a free download of the destination's corresponding eBook. It is available now from the free Walking Eye container app in the App Store and Google Play. Simply download the Walking Eye container app to access the eBook dedicated to your purchased book. The app also features free information on local events taking place and activities you can enjoy during your stay, with the option to book them. In addition, premium content for a wide range of other destinations is available to purchase in-app.

'MAGIC' BEACH
The best of many on the island's south coast.
See page 50.

VOLCANIC CALDERA
Sulphurous marvel at the heart of Nísyros.
See page 62.

SUNSET BEHIND TÉLENDOS
See the princess profile – or a snail. See page 72.

ITALIAN ARCHITECTURE
On Kos, Kálymnos and Léros. See page 75.

SCUBA DIVING IN LÉROS
A rich trove of war debris. See page 85.

AGÍOU IOÁNNOU THEOLÓGOU MONASTERY
The crowning glory of Pátmos, frescoed and treasured. See page 80.

A PERFECT TOUR

Day 1

First swim
At Kos airport, pick up hire car, driving straight to a seafood meal in Kardámena or Mastihári. Have a refreshing swim off Polémi or Psilós Gremós beach before hotel check-in at Kos Town, Psalídi or Ágios Fokás.

Day 4

A climb and a soak
Try more advanced windsurfing near Cape Psalídi, before lunch at Old Pyli taverna in Amanioú. Afterwards, see Lagoúdi village's frescoed church before climbing Khristós peak in the late afternoon. Dinner at Ziá's Oromedon taverna; then drive to Bros Thermá hot springs to assuage aches and pains.

Day 2

Kos Town
Explore the Knights' Neratziá castle in the morning, then the Casa Romana museum. Swim near Tingáki or Marmári before lunch in or near Tingáki. Visit the hillside Asklepion in the late afternoon, before dinner at a Platáni taverna.

Day 3

Southwest coast
See the Archaeological Museum before driving to Andimáhia's castle followed by lunch at Liminónas. Continue to the far southwest around Kéfalos. Spend sunset on a horseback ride from the Salt Lake stables. Dinner is at Ambavris Taverna, outside town.

Day 5

Nísyros
Take a morning excursion boat to Nísyros, where you overnight. On a scooter, visit its volcanic caldera, Pahiá Ámmos beach, the archaeological museum, two castles and two inland villages. Have lunch in Emborió, dinner in Mandráki or Lakkí, and visit the thermal baths.

Day 7

Tiny Psérimos

Take the daily caique from Póthia harbour to Psérimos islet, with its idyllic beaches and laid-back pace; lunch at Avlákia port. Evening return to Kálymnos, with dinner in Póthia.

Day 10

Back to Kos

Take the morning catamaran from Pátmos to Kos, arriving in time for your afternoon or evening flight home. Use any spare time in Kos Town.

Day 6

Kálymnos

Board the catamaran from Nísyros to Kálymnos, arriving at lunchtime. From your Póthia base, head for Myrtiés by bus or scooter and take a little boat to peaceful Télendos islet. Return to Kálymnos to enjoy the sunset from a west-coast taverna at Linariá or Armeós.

Day 8

Léros

Pop into Póthia's Archaeological Museum then get the catamaran to Léros, arriving for lunch at Dimitris O Karaflas after hiring a scooter. Have an afternoon swim and a look at Lakkí's Italian monuments, then head up to the Knights' castle for superb sunset views. Dinner in Krithóni or Vromólithos.

Day 9

Pátmos

Visit the Álinda Historical/Folklore museum before mid-day catamaran to Pátmos, with a swim and lunch at a beach and then an atmospheric evening pilgrimage to Hóra's magnificent monastery. Dinner at Tzivaeri in Skála.

CONTENTS

INTRODUCTION

It is impossible not to feel the weight of history when you arrive in Kos. The marble of Hellenistic and Roman sites, the sandstone of medieval churches and castles, are all tangible legacies of a long history. However, to imagine that Kos only appeals to archaeology buffs would be a mistake. With long, hot summer days, a balmy sea lapping numerous beaches, and lots to do, the island is a holidaymakers' paradise.

Kos belongs to the Dodecanese, an archipelago scattered in the southeastern Aegean Sea between Greece and Turkey. Originally made up of twelve major islands (*dódeka nisiá* means 'twelve islands' in Greek) that coordinated action against Ottoman repression during the late 19th and early 20th centuries, the group is now an administrative sub-region of Greece comprising several dozen islands and islets, though only twenty have permanent inhabitants.

Admiring the view from the Asklepion

Kos ranks third among the Dodecanese in size – but second in population at 33,388 – and has been settled since ancient times, thanks to wide fertile plains, and a good harbour opposite Asia Minor, just three nautical miles away. The island is roughly 40km/24.7 miles long, 11km/6 miles wide at the thickest point, 287.2 sq km/111 sq miles in area, and orientated northeast to southwest on its long axis. Its coastline, a mix of sheer cliffs or beach, measures 112km/70 miles. Sand dunes are stabilised by important groves of strictly protected sea juniper (*Juniperus macrocarpa*), in Greek *kédros* and thus invariably, wrongly translated as 'cedar'. There are more junipers, and pines, up on the central mountain. Geologically, Kos is of partly volcanic origin (in the southwest), and rose from the seabed in stages between 1 million and 158,000 years ago. There are important wetlands at Alykí and Psalídi, which attract dozens of species of migrating birds annually.

Kos has always been a 'breadbasket' island, with a very limited maritime tradition, and could still be agriculturally self-sustaining if the need arose. In antiquity, Kos was renowned for its silk and wine; the silk industry is long gone, but wine-making has recently revived with a bang, and tasting local bottlings should be part of any visit. Unlike many holiday islands, farming has not completely been elbowed aside – herds of cattle grazing amidst wire-bound bales of hay are still very much part of the landscape, and local cheese is quite esteemed.

The melon island

Near Linopótis, roadside stalls sell melons. The island has always been famous for watermelons especially, formerly exporting them in quantity to other parts of Greece. Old-timers on barren nearby islets remember, as children, eagerly awaiting the arrival of the summer watermelon boats from Kos.

Kos was never strong enough to rule itself, but desirable and strategically located enough to be coveted by every east-Mediterranean empire or nearby state. It has, by turns, been part of the Dorian Hexapolis, the Achaemenid Persian Empire, Athens' Delian Confederacy, ancient Karya, the Alexandria-based Ptolemaic kingdom, the Roman republic and empire, Byzantium, Crusader principalities, the Ottoman Empire, the Italian 'Islands of the Aegean', and only since 1948 the modern Greek state. Each of these possessors from the Ptolemies onwards have left their mark on the island. Uneasy relations with adjacent Turkey mean that Kos has been heavily garrisoned by Greece since the 1950s, and when touring you shouldn't be surprised to see tanks or armoured vehicles

REFUGEES AND KOS

Kos spent much of 2015 in the media spotlight as the destination of some of the 200,000 migrants who arrived in Greece by sea through September. At one point there were 7,500 refugees – mostly Syrian but also Iraqi and Afghan – on Kos, some housed in disused hotels but otherwise sleeping rough. Each summer day, up to another thousand landed on rubber rafts, abandoned (along with life-vests) on assorted beaches. Greece overall, and Kos in particular, was unable to cope; mid-economic crisis, the country simply hadn't the resources to house and feed so many unexpected guests, and received scant assistance from the EU. On Kos (and other islands), sympathetic foreigners brought in supplies or took up local collections to feed and clothe the refugees, many of them women and children.

The immigrants, neither aggressive nor importunate towards tourists, shouldn't affect your holiday plans; all efforts are made to transfer them to Piraeus and the Lávrio refugee camp as soon as possible.

exercising in the volcanic badlands and ravines near the airport, or parked in ranks at nearby military bases. Of late, better relations, and Greece's budgetary distress, mean that the military presence is rather scaled down – and you are as likely to see Turkish civilian holidaymakers as any other.

Kos harbour

KOS OF THE TOURISTS

The Italians built the first hotel on Kos in 1928, but British mass tourism arrived (at Kardámena) only during the 1970s, something observed wryly in John Ebdon's long-out-of-print but easy to obtain *Ebdon's Iliad*. The Dutch 'pioneered' the northern section of Kos Town, as well as the 'bar lanes' at Mandráki, during the 1980s, and to some extent have remained loyal to it. Italians, Belgians and Germanophones were next; an increasing orientation towards the family and convention markets was signalled by the opening of many all-inclusive resorts around the millennium. Russians appeared just after that, but their numbers have now dropped as sanctions against Putin's regime shred the ruble's value. Cross-border tourism is increasingly significant, with potential Turkish visitors helped by the fact that the crossing from Bodrum opposite is the cheapest and most reliable for any of Greece's frontier islands.

For much of the 1980s and 1990s, Kos had a bad press, derided for being flat and boring – the centre of the island is indeed so low-lying that the peak of Nísyros can be glimpsed above it from Kálymnos to the north – as well as for its alleged

View from the Ágios Stéfanos basilica to Kéfalos beach

lack of architectural or culinary distinction. Clearly those deriders hadn't seen forested central Mt Díkeos or the rugged Kéfalos peninsula, Kos' unique Italian architectural heritage, or tasted the – by Greek island standards – highly idiosyncratic local cuisine, dishing up everything from Turkish-style kebabs to candied tomatoes to wine-marinated cheese to pork brawn.

In fact Kos has a lot to boast about: tourism here has long been handled uncharacteristically efficiently, courtesy of a well-developed infrastructure: the urban bus service is a marvel, cyclists and the disabled are actively catered for with a network of marked bicycle lanes and wheelchair ramps in and around Kos Town, and proudly signposted biological sewage plants at Psalídi and Kardámena have had a salutary effect on island seawater quality.

Twenty-first-century Kos remains one of the most popular islands with package holidaymakers, thanks to its many fine beaches, castles, and nightlife, as well as strong air links to northern Europe. With no university faculty (unlike many other large Greek islands) and no industry to speak of, tourism is the linchpin of the local economy. This is even more critical now given the country's economic tailspin in other respects, and you will be welcomed with open arms.

A BRIEF HISTORY

PREHISTORIC BEGINNINGS

The earliest habitation on Kos dates to 3400 BC, at the Asprí
Pétra cave; Kalymnian caverns hosted Neolithic man 2,000
years earlier. Early and Middle Bronze-Age settlers preferred
Kos's fertile plains, with the exception of a Minoan expedition
which founded the Seraglio site near the only natural harbour.
After Minoan civilisation collapsed around 1400 BC, Mycenean
colonists took over Seraglio, staying until the arrival of the
'Sea Peoples' from beyond the Black Sea three centuries later.

The Seraglio was re-inhabited in about 900 BC by Argolid
Dorians, who introduced the worship of Asklepios. Soon Kos
entered history as a member of the Dorian Hexapolis, a fed-
eration of six cities on Rhodes, Kos and Anatolia opposite.

PERSIANS TO ROMANS

The Achaemenid Persian Empire under Cyrus the Great conquered Anatolia soon after 546 BC; Kos came briefly under
Persian control, towards 500 BC. After Greek victories over the
Persians at Plataea and Mykale in 479 BC, the island joined
the Athenian-dominated Delian Confederacy. Kos got caught
up in the Peloponnesian War of 431–404 BC, between Athens,
Sparta and their respective allies; despite being Dorian, it did
not join the Spartan side until 412 BC. Athens retaliated with
a punitive expedition, but Kos again revolted in 407, before
returning to the Athenian fold in 378. A civil war between pro-
Spartan and pro-Athenian factions on Kos was only averted
by the 366 BC founding of a new city, near Seraglio, and the
political subservience or abandonment of other island towns.

Kos city, with its excellent harbour near the main Aegean
sea-lane, prospered. After brief rule by Halikarnassos opposite, both cities were taken by Alexander the Great's general,
Ptolemy, in 333 BC, and for the next 150 years Kos had strong

Fresco inside the Monastery of St John the Theologian, Pátmos

links to the Ptolemaic capital, Alexandria.

Kos supported Rome during its 215–190 BC campaigns on the Greek mainland to crush the last Macedonian kings, and became a prominent banking centre. In 88 BC, Mithridates of Pontus sacked Kos; in revenge Kos provided a fleet to Rome, and was thus conspicuously favoured under both the Roman Republic and Empire, when it served as a popular resort for cures at the Asklepion.

BYZANTIUM AND CHRISTIANITY

The declining Roman Empire was divided into eastern and western empires. In 330 AD, eastern Emperor Constantine moved his capital to Byzantium, renaming it Constantinople (modern Istanbul) after him. While the last western emperor was deposed by Goths in 476, this eastern portion became the dominant east-Mediterranean power until 1025.

By 393, Christianity was the state religion; its liturgies and New Testament were written in *koine* Greek, based on Alexandria's Hellenistic dialect. Byzantine authorities eradicated any traces of pagan Hellenism, most obviously by recycling temple masonry when building churches.

Christianity came early to the Dodecanese. Kos, plus many smaller islands, have ruined basilicas with elaborate floors, invariably from the fifth or sixth century, often built atop pagan temples; these basilicas were either levelled by a severe earthquake/tsunami in 554 AD, or by the Saracen raids of the following century.

The 600s saw Constantinople besieged by Persians and Arabs, but the Byzantine Empire survived, losing only Egypt. From the ninth through the early eleventh centuries, in the Byzantine heartland, Orthodox Byzantine faith exhibited a spiritual confidence, seeing Constantinople as a 'new Jerusalem' for the 'chosen people'. This prompted disastrous diplomatic and ecclesiastical conflict with the Catholic West, culminating in the 1054 schism.

Meanwhile, the Dodecanese became a backwater subject to periodic pirate raids, figuring little in history except for the 1088 foundation of Agíou Ioánnou Theológou monastery on

HIPPOKRATES, FATHER OF MEDICINE

Hippokrates (c.460–370 BC) is regarded as the father of scientific medicine, and still influences doctors today through the Hippocratic oath – which he probably didn't compose, and scarcely resembles its original form. Hippokrates was definitely born on Kos, probably at ancient Astypalaia, but other details of his life are obscure. He was certainly a great healer who travelled throughout Classical Greece, but spent part of his career teaching and practising on his native island. Around seventy medical texts have been attributed to Hippokrates, only a few of which could he have personally written. *Airs, Waters and Places*, a treatise on the importance of environment for health from about 400 BC, is reckoned to be his, but most others were probably a compilation from a Kos library, which later surfaced in Ptolemean Alexandria during the second century BC. This emphasis on good air and water, and the holistic approach of ancient Greek medicine, seems positively modern. His native island duly honours him today, with a tree, a street, a park, a statue and an international medical institute named after him.

Mehmet II's troops laying siege to Constantinople in 1453

Pátmos, a previously insignificant island granted to Abbot Khristodoulos by the emperor.

CRUSADER AND OTTOMAN CONQUEST

In 1095, Norman crusaders raided the Dodecanese en route to Jerusalem. Worse followed in 1204, when Venetians, Franks and Germans diverted the Fourth Crusade, sacking and occupying Constantinople. Latin princes and their followers divided up choice parts of the empire. Byzantium was reduced to four small peripheral kingdoms *(despotates)*; none was based in the islands, though Rhodes and Kos were held by Leo Gabalas, a Byzantine aristocrat, for four decades.

In 1261, the Paleologos dynasty, provisionally based at Nicaea, recovered Constantinople but little of its former territory and power. Their only Latin allies were the Genoese, whose support came at a price: extensive commercial privileges in the capital, and the ceding, at various moments up to 1355, of many Aegean islands to assorted Genoese families.

Genoese adventurers had seized Rhodes and other Dodecanese islands by 1248, but in 1309 the crusading Knights Hospitallers of St John, expelled from Palestine and dissatisfied on Cyprus, conquered Rhodes. Genoese Kós fell to the Knights in 1314, after which their possession of most of the Dodecanese was guaranteed. Astypálea, Kárpathos and Kásos stayed Venetian, while Pátmos remained Orthodox monastic territory. Knightly citadels, either purpose-built or adapted Byzantine castles, appeared on most islands.

The Byzantines faced a much stronger threat than the crusaders in the expanding Ottoman Turkish Empire. Weakened by internal struggles, they proved no match for the Turks. On 29 May 1453, Constantinople fell to Sultan Mehmet II after a seven-week siege.

From their strongholds, the Knights engaged in both legitimate trade and piracy, constituting a major irritant to the expanding Ottoman Empire. Attempts to dislodge them from Kos in 1457 and 1477 failed; it took the six-month siege of Rhodes in 1522 by Sultan Süleyman the Magnificent to compel their surrender and cession of all the Dodecanese islands.

Under Ottoman rule, the Dodecanese lapsed into a conservative mode of village life. Only larger islands with flat, arable land, like Rhodes and Kos, attracted extensive Muslim colonisation and garrisoning, primarily in the largest towns, where non-Muslims were forbidden residence in the strategic central citadels. Taxes and discipline were imposed through imperial

Calming effect of Kos

The Fourth Earl of Sandwich, doing his 1738 Grand Tour, noted that 'the Turks of Kos are... endued with more affability than the mahometans in any other part of the Levant,' while an 1815 visitor observed that 'The Turks are by no means rigid or savage, and marry with the Greeks by civil contract.'

judges, tax collectors and military personnel, but local notables retained large enterprises or estates. Generally, insular Ottoman government was lackadaisical; 18th- and 19th-century travellers reported extensive neglect on Rhodes, including discarded weapons and unrepaired damage from the 1522 siege.

Greek identity was preserved through the Orthodox Church, which, despite occasional enforced conversion and inter-marriage, suffered little interference from the Ottomans. All Orthodox peoples, Greek or otherwise, were considered one *millet* (subject nation), their patriarch responsible for his flock's behaviour, tax collection and administering communal and inheritance law. Monasteries organised primary schooling – and on Pátmos, a distinguished secondary academy.

Smaller islands enjoyed significant autonomy and special concessions (particularly tax exemption) under Ottoman rule. These privileges were honoured even after the establishment of a Greek state in 1830, withdrawn incrementally only after 1874. Barren maritime Dodecanesian islands made fortunes either through sponge-diving, transporting Anatolian goods with their own fleets, or building boats on Turkish commission. Until the 18th century, the Ottomans never acquired much seamanship, relying instead on Aegean crews and shipyards.

ITALIAN RULE AND WORLD WAR II

The Dodecanese were seized by Italy in a brief, spring 1912 campaign, part of an ongoing war to expel the Ottomans from Libya. At first Greek Orthodox islanders acclaimed the Italians as liberators, who promised not to outstay their welcome. Early in World War I, however, Italy remained neutral, and was only persuaded to join the Entente by being promised, among other things, that its sovereignty over the Dodecanese would be rec-ognised. Between 1915 and 1923, international conferences agreed that (except for Rhodes) the Dodecanese would be given to Greece, but after the collapse of Greece's Asia Minor invasion, and the rise of Italian Fascism, this became unlikely.

In 1923, Italy definitively annexed the Dodecanese as the *Isole Italiane del'Egeo*, embarking upon gradual, forced Latinisation. During the term of first Governor Mario Lago, land was expropriated for Italian colonists and intermarriage with local Greeks encouraged, though only Catholic ceremonies were valid. A puppet Orthodox archbishopric was set up, and when this failed (except for three collaborationist bishops), the Orthodox rite was suppressed completely. Italian was introduced as the compulsory language of public life in 1936, when ardently Fascist Cesare Maria de Vecchi replaced Lago and accelerated assimilationist measures. These provoked riots on Kálymnos (with stone-throwing women in the front line).

Italian architecture in Lakkí, Léros

The Dodecanese were never part of Italy: islanders were awarded en masse 'lesser' Italian nationality, with no obligation for military service (and no civic rights), while 'major' or full Italian citizenship was granted to those who collaborated conspicuously with the authorities. Emigration was possible on a 'minor' passport, and indeed by 1939 the Greek population of many islands had halved, which the Fascists probably intended.

Expatriated Dodecanesians formed pressure groups in New York, Egypt, Australia and England to lobby any interested audience about the Greekness of the Dodecanese.

On larger islands, massive public works were undertaken to make them showcases of this 'Italian Aegean Empire'; roads, monumental buildings and waterworks were constructed (often with forced Greek labour), sound and unsound archaeology engaged in, and accurate mapping done. The first hotels rose on Rhodes and Kós; the first tourists arrived by boat or seaplane. However, smaller islands, except for militarised Léros, were neglected.

Using a submarine dispatched from Léros, the Italians torpedoed the Greek cruiser *Elli* on 15 August 1940. This outrage went unanswered, as Greece was unprepared for war; but when Mussolini overran Albania, and on 28 October sent an ultimatum demanding passage for his troops through Greece, Greek dictator Metaxas responded to the Italian ambassador in Athens with the apocryphal *"óhi"* (no). (In fact, his answer, in mutually understood French, was *"Alors, c'est la guerre"* – a gesture still celebrated as a national holiday.)

Greece was defeated in April 1941 and a tripartite German-Bulgarian-Italian occupation imposed; little changed in the Dodecanese, except that Governor De Vecchi – hated even by many Italians – was replaced by Admiral Inigo Campioni.

When Italy capitulated on 8 September 1943, a brief free-for-all ensued on the Greek islands it had controlled. Churchill considered the Dodecanese easy pickings, but was denied assistance by the US, reluctant to endanger its precarious advance through Italy. The British occupied Kós and Léros, but insufficiently to repel German counterattacks; Kos fell on 3 October, Léros on 16 November, with considerable losses. German troops imprisoned and executed their erstwhile Italian allies, particularly on Rhodes, Léros and Kos.

Nazi tanks in Rhodes, August 1943

The British gradually took the Dodecanese from September 1944 onwards, picking off islands one by one, though Rhodes, Kos and Léros were too strongly defended and only abandoned by the Germans after their May 1945 surrender to the Allies, signed on Dodecanesian Sými. Along with western Crete, these were the last territories they held.

The British stayed for 22 months from May 1945, causing considerable unease in the Greek government, which suspected that they meant to set up a Cyprus-style colony or (worse) hand some or all of the Dodecanese back to Turkey. However, the British claimed they intended to cede these islands to Greece once it became clear the central government would prevail against communist rebels on the mainland, and were also awaiting the outcome of the Italian-Greek peace treaty negotiations.

The negotiations' main sticking points were Greek demands for war reparations versus Italian claims of compensation for 'improvements' to the Dodecanese (finally deemed to offset each other) and, more seriously, the fate of native Italians, and Greeks with 'major' Italian nationality. Metropolitan Italians, including those married to islanders, were given a year from February 1947 to choose between Greek or Italian nationality; if the latter, they were obliged to leave for Italy (a large number stayed). Native islanders who enjoyed 'major' Italian citizenship had their cases examined minutely; those who had adopted this status enthusiastically were also deported to Italy.

Once the treaty was ratified, the Greek Army assumed control on 31 March. A military governor presided over a ten-month lustration regime, evaluating the cases of 'major' Italian subjects, and winkling out any communists. Once this was completed, the Dodecanese were officially annexed by Greece on 9 January 1948, and the first civilian governor appointed.

Sponge divers in Kálymnos, 1955

UNION WITH GREECE

A demoralised, impoverished Greece entered the American/ NATO orbit during the 1950s. This and the next decade also saw wholesale emigration abroad or internally to larger cities. In the Dodecanese, many inhabitants of Kos and Kálymnos in particular headed off to Australia or Canada, both countries with labour shortages and less bothered about left-wing political affiliation than the US. As relations with neighbouring Turkey worsened after 1954, the resulting sense of insecurity on border islands accelerated depopulation.

Tourism saved some islands from complete desertion, though it began gradually. Kálymnos, Léros and Pátmos saw significant tourism only from the late 1980s onwards. The centre-left PASOK government, first elected in 1981 and in power almost uninterruptedly until 2004, tended to favour remote islands (which voted accordingly), and the infrastructure on Kos improved notably. Unusual continuity in local administration also helped, with an efficient mayor re-elected repeatedly.

THE BAILOUT YEARS

After being in opposition since 2004, PASOK defeated centre-right Néa Dimokratía (ND) in 2009, with George Papandreou becoming prime minister. He soon discovered that the outgoing ND government had minimised the extent of Greece's national debt, and budget deficit. In 2010 the first bailout from European and international lenders was solicited. It merely enabled Greece to continue making payments to creditors. By late 2011, despite imposition of the harshest austerity measures seen in post-1945 Europe, Greece's economy and Papandreou's position had both become untenable; Papandreou resigned in favour of a six-month technocratic government of national unity.

Successive elections of May and June 2012 produced hung parliaments, with ND the top-finishing party in both. A coalition, expressly to impose more creditor-demanded austerity and manage a second bailout, was assembled from ND, PASOK and centre-left DIMAR, specifically excluding new upstart leftist party SYRIZA. By late 2014, the result was clear: a collapsing economy with droves of small and medium-sized businesses bankrupted, overall unemployment reaching 27 percent, a 57-percent youth unemployment rate, and massive emigration of young, skilled individuals.

ND Prime Minister Antonis Samaras' favoured candidate for president, elected by parliament, failed to secure a majority in December 2014. Constitutionally mandatory elections were set for 25 January 2015. In these, SYRIZA, under charismatic leader Alexis Tsipras, gained a plurality but not a majority of parliamentary seats. Their platform had promised to square the circle of easing austerity while remaining within the eurozone. The only other party willing to enter into a coalition with SYRIZA was anti-EU, anti-bailout, far-right ANEL. In any case, the old ND-PASOK duopoly was finished.

Negotiations resumed with Greece's creditors with a view to a third bailout. Bad faith, especially by German Finance Minister Wolfgang Schäuble and his Greek counterpart Ioannis Varoufakis, were abundantly evident on both sides. Talks were suspended in late June, just before PM Tsipras announced a 5 July referendum on the terms of the bailout offered, and ordered Greece's banks shut for three weeks and ATM withdrawal limits imposed to prevent them from collapsing.

The referendum went massively against accepting another bailout on the terms of the creditors, who had made it clear that their offer had already been withdrawn. Despite this, Tsipras soon caved in and accepted a third bailout even harsher than the one rejected. Battling rebels within his own party, he only secured approval of this €86 billion deal with opposition support. Added to its existing debts, Greece would now owe over €400 billion with no hope of ever paying it off.

The rebels quickly formed their own party, and Tsipras resigned prior to elections held on 20 September. Defying predictions of deadlock with ND, these produced another resounding plurality for SYRIZA, which (to the consternation of many) renewed the coalition with ANEL. But Greece's sovereignty has been sharply curtailed; all social and financial policies will be essentially dictated by an EU task force until further notice.

HISTORICAL LANDMARKS

3400 BC Neolithic settlement at Asprí Pétra, Kos.

1620 BC Minoans colonise Seraglio site, Kos.

850 BC Kos becomes a member of the Dorian Hexapolis.

460–370 BC Hippokrates's approximate lifetime.

366 BC Ancient Kos established on the site of the present town; Asklepion founded.

Late 3rd century BC – early 2nd century BC Kos is ruled from Ptolemaic Alexandria.

88 BC Pro-Roman Kos sacked by Mithridates of Pontos.

325 AD Kos already ranks as a bishopric.

554 AD Severe earthquake and tsunami wrecks Kos.

c. 1314 Knights Hospitaller of St John assume control of Kos, Nísyros, Kálymnos and Léros from the Genoese.

1523 Knights evacuate peacefully following the successful Ottoman siege of Rhodes.

1912 Italians oust Ottomans from Kos and all other Dodecanese isles.

1923–43 Systematic archaeological excavations on Kos; Italian urban renewal and monuments on Kos, Kálymnos and Léros.

1933 Severe earthquake levels much of Kos Town.

1940 Italy attacks Greece; Léros is a vital Italian base.

1943 Germans seize control of the Dodecanese from the Italians, and defeat the British in the battles of Kos and Léros.

1945 Germany surrenders Kos, Léros and Rhodes to the British.

1947 British cede the Dodecanese to a Greek military governor.

1950s–60s Large-scale emigration to Australia and Canada.

1970s Beginning of Kos mass tourism.

2009–14 Incoming government discovers Greece is bankrupt; EU-brokered bailouts begin but economy contracts 25 percent over five years.

2015 SYRIZA-dominated coalition government elected, fraught negotiations with creditors produce third bailout. Second elections in September result in a second SYRIZA-ANEL coalition and the eclipse of SYRIZA radicals.

WHERE TO GO

Kos is an easy island to explore, with good public transport for independent sightseeing, as well as abundant outlets for renting cars, scooters or push-bikes. There's no need to take an organised tour.

This guide explores Kos Town first. Next there's a tour around the island, starting with Platáni and the nearby Asklepion, then continuing around the coastline before forays into the interior. Finally there are excursions to (or more rewardingly, overnight stays on) a half-dozen smaller nearby islands.

KOS TOWN

Minoan settlers were attracted by Kos's only good natural harbour, opposite ancient Halikarnassos (modern Bodrum), and despite regular, devastating earthquakes throughout its history, **Kos Town** ❶ has remained there, prospering from seaborne trade. The contemporary city spreads in all directions from almost landlocked Mandráki port. Apart from the imposing Knights Hospitaller's castle, the first thing visible arriving by sea, its most compelling attractions are abundant Hellenistic and Roman ruins, many only revealed by a 1933 earthquake, and some quirky Italian architecture.

Despite a population of 19,432 – well over half the islanders – Kos Town feels uncluttered, thanks to its sprawling, flat layout. Areas of open space alternate with a hotchpotch of archaeological zones, surviving Ottoman quarters, and Italian-built mock-medieval, Rationalist and Art Deco-ish buildings, designed in two phases (1926–1929 and 1934–1939) either side of the earthquake by architects Florestano di Fausto, Rodolfo Petracco and Armando Bernabiti. Plans incorporated, as always, a Foro Italico, the Italian administrative complex close

The ruins of the Roman Agora and the Loggia Mosque, Kos Town

to the castle, and a Casa del Fascio (Fascist Headquarters), with the inevitable speaker's tower for haranguing party rallies gathered on the central square below. The maze-like Ottoman core aside, this is a planned town, with pines and shrubbery planted by the Italians now fully matured, especially in the garden suburb extending east of the centre, its worker and officer housing mostly the work of **Mario Paolini**.

NERATZIÁ CASTLE

An obvious first stop is **Neratziá Castle (Castle of the Knights)** Ⓐ (June–Sept Tue–Sun 8am–6.40pm, Oct–May 8am–2.40pm; charge), reached by a causeway over its former moat. The

Tumbled columns in Neratziá Castle

moat was long ago filled and planted with palms *(fínikes)* – thus the avenue's Greek name, Finíkon. The original Knights' castle which stood here from 1314 until 1450 has vanished without trace, replaced by the existing inner castle (1450–78). This nestles within an outer citadel, built to formidable thickness between 1495 and 1514 to withstand advances in artillery technology following unsuccessful Ottoman sieges in 1457 and 1477. The fortification walls make an excellent vantage point for photographs over **Mandráki**.

A fair proportion of ancient Kos, as masonry fragments

and tumbled columns, has been incorporated into the walls of both strongholds or, more recently, piled up loose in the southeast forecourt. Escutcheons and coats-of-arms on various walls and towers will appeal to heraldry aficionados, as the period of construction spanned the terms of several Grand Masters and local governors

> **Signs of Life**
>
> The biggest explosion that ever occurred at Neratziá castle was orchestrated for the finale of Werner Herzog's black-and-white first feature film, *Signs of Life* (1968), in which a low-ranking Wehrmacht soldier goes berserk in 1944 and torches an ammunition dump inside the castle.

of the Knights. The south corner of the older castle, for example, bears two Grand Masters' escutcheons, best admired from the massive, most technically advanced southwest bastion, identified with Grand Master Fabrizio del Caretto, who finished the job. Dozens of cannonballs lie about, few if any fired in anger, since this castle surrendered peacefully in accordance with the terms ending the marathon 1522 siege of Rhodes.

HIPPOKRATES' PLANE TREE AND THE LOGGIA MOSQUE

Steel scaffolding has replaced the ancient pillars that once propped up sagging branches of **Hippokrates' plane tree**, immediately opposite the causeway leading into Neratziá castle. At seven hundred years of age, this venerable tree has a fair claim to being among the oldest in the Mediterranean, though it's not really elderly enough to have seen the great healer himself. The trunk has split into four sections, which in any other species would presage imminent demise, but abundant root-suckers promise continuation. Adjacent stand a hexagonal Turkish pillar fountain, another fountain draining into an ancient sarcophagus (neither running now), and the imposing 1786-built mosque of Gazi Hasan Pasha, better known as the **Loggia Mosque** ⓑ after its covered northern portico. The upper two stories are locked and window tracery still bears marks of wartime bombardment. The ground floor – like that of its contemporary (1780) the **Defterdar Mosque** on nearby Platía Eleftherías – is occupied by tourist-orientated shops. This is not sacrilegious desecration, but common Ottoman practice; the shopkeepers' rent goes towards the upkeep of the mosque overhead.

THE ANCIENT TOWN

The largest excavated section of ancient Kos is the **agora** ⓒ, a sunken zone (unrestricted access) reached from either Ippokrátous or Nafklírou streets. The latter, a pedestrian lane (and lately much-subdued nightlife mecca), is separated from Platía Eleftherías by the **Pórta tou Fórou** ⓓ, all that remains of the outer city walls which the Knights erected between 1391 and 1396.

What you see is confusing and jumbled owing to successive earthquakes in 142, 469 and 554 AD; the most salient items are the foundations of a massive double Aphrodite sanctuary roughly in the centre of the site, some columns of a Hellenistic stoa near the Loggia Mosque, plus two re-erected columns and the architrave of the Roman agora itself, on the far west.

Another, more comprehensible section of the ancient town, the **western excavations** ⓔ (unrestricted access), abuts the ancient acropolis – where Platía Diagóras lies today. Intersecting marble-paved **Roman streets** (Cardo and Decumana), dating from the third century AD, lend definition to this area, as does the **Xystós**, or colonnade, of a covered running track. Inside the Xystós the hulking brick ruins of a bath squat alongside the original arch of its furnace room. South of the Xystós stands the restored door-frame of a baptistry belonging to a Christian basilica erected above the baths after 469 AD. The floor of the

Statuary inside the Archaeological Museum

basilica, as well as that of an unidentified building at the north-ern end of the excavations, retain well-preserved mosaic frag-ments, although the best have been carted off to Rhodes. What remains tends to be under several inches of protective gravel or off-limits to visitors, like the famous **Europa mosaic** house to the north of Decumana street – though it, plus others nearby showing gladiators, a boar being speared and sundry gods or muses, can be viewed from a distance.

Secreted in a cypress grove across Grigoríou tou Pémptou Street is a fourteen-row Roman **odeion** ❻, which in ancient times hosted musical events associated with the *Asklepieia* festivals (see page 40); it was re-clad in new marble during 1999–2000 and again is a popular concert venue.

ARCHAEOLOGICAL MUSEUM
The north side of Platía Eleftherías is dominated by the newly refurbished **Archaeological Museum** ❼ (Tue–Sun 8.30am–2.40pm; charge), designed and built in 1935 in severe Rationalist

style by Rodolfo Petracco. The Italians' original choice of exhibits was a none-too-subtle propaganda exercise, with a distinct Latin bias. Four galleries containing good, if not superlative, statuary are grouped around a central atrium where a Roman mosaic shows Hippokrates welcoming Asklepios to Kos. The most famous exhibit, a statue thought to portray Hippokrates, is in fact Hellenistic, as is a vividly coloured, fragmentary fish mosaic at the rear of the atrium. But most of the other highly regarded works – Hermes seated with a lamb, Artemis hunting, Hygeia offering an egg to Asklepios' serpent, a boxer with his arms bound in rope, statues of wealthy townspeople – are emphatically Roman.

THE CASA ROMANA

The **Casa Romana** $\bullet$ (Tue–Sun 10am–5.40pm; free), at the south edge of town, re-opened in 2015 after a five-year refit, well worth the wait; it now effectively functions as a museum of domestic, late-Roman (3rd–4th centuries AD) life. During World War II it served as an Italian infirmary – until 2010 you could still see faded red crosses painted on the exterior to deter Allied bombers.

The structure, devastated by the 554 AD earthquake but abandoned long before, was evidently the villa of a wealthy family, arrayed around three atria with third-century tessellated marble or **mosaic floors**. The mosaic closest to the ticket booth shows a lion and a leopard respectively mauling two stags; the largest courtyard to the south is flanked by rooms, on opposite sides, depicting another panther and a tiger; while the pool of the third atrium is surrounded by dolphins, fish and two leaping leopards, plus a damaged nymph riding a horse-headed sea-monster, possibly a representation of Poseidon. Standouts amongst the small finds displayed are a relief of a *nekrodeipno* (funerary banquet) with the goddess Kybele presiding; a figurine of Venus adjusting her sandal; and elaborate 'Knidos-style' oil-lamps.

THE OTTOMAN OLD TOWN: HALUVAZIÁ

Kos's medieval 'old town', the former Muslim district of **Haluvaziá ❶**, lines either side of a pedestrianised street running from behind the Italian-era market hall on Platía Eleftherías as far as Platía Diagóras and the orphaned minaret of the earthquake-tumbled Yeni Kapı Mosque overlooking the western excavations. It was long considered an undesira-

Café life in Platía Eleftherías

ble area, but while all the rickety townhouses nearby collapsed in the 1933 earthquake, the sturdily built stone dwellings and shops here survived. Today, they are crammed with superfluous tourist boutiques, cafés and tavernas; one of the few genuinely old things here is a dry **Turkish fountain** with an Ottoman inscription, found where the walkway cobbles cross Venizélou. Another juts out from the wall of the barber shop at the corner of Hristodoúlou and Passanikoláki, next to the minaret-less but still-functioning **Atik Mosque** (refurbished in the 19th century), whose name means 'Mosque of the Freed Slaves'.

ITALIAN MONUMENTS

If you're at all interested in local Italian monuments, a worthwhile first stop is the well-done display **'The Creation of the**

Casa del Fascio

New Town of Kos' (daily 10am–10pm; charge), housed appropriately enough in the former Italian-built veterinary compound. Photos and documents chart Italian social policy, the 1933 earthquake's aftermath, prominent architects, and their best buildings.

The seafront Foro Italico extending southeast from Neratziá castle, erected during 1927–29, comprises the local **administration building**, now the police station; the adjoining courthouse, still in use; the graceful **Albergo Gelsomino** ❿, abandoned and in poor repair; the mayor's residence, today the municipal cultural centre; the **Italian officers' club**, now the Avra Lounge Bar; and inland opposite **Evangelismós Church** ⓚ, originally the Catholic cathedral of Agnus Dei. From the same era, but on the far side of the harbour entrance, stands the crenellated **power plant**, with the **town hall** found en route, behind Aktí Koundouriótou.

Post-earthquake monuments are more scattered, dating mostly from 1934–35. Notable ones include the **Casa del Fascio** ⓛ (today part-occupied by the winter Orfeas cinema) with its prominent clock-tower/speaker's balcony; the **covered market** ⓜ or *dimotikí agorá*, a fun if expensive place to souvenir-shop; and the aforementioned archaeological museum – all flanking focal Platía Eleftherías. Further afield are the exceptionally eclectic **synagogue** ⓝ at Alexándrou Diakoú 4; the round-fronted, seafront **primary school** ⓞ, at the base of Kanári; the **Fascist Youth building** ⓟ at the corner of Venizélou and Koraí, now a branch of Pireos Bank; and the circular 1937 **Amnós tou Theoú** ⓠ (Agnus Dei) Catholic church. Many other mixed-use buildings pop up around town, with shops on the ground floor and residences upstairs. Much of the fun in strolling around is spotting them – there's a particularly extravagant one at the corner of Venizélou and Vasiléos Pávlou.

PLATÁNI AND THE ASKLEPION

The Greek–Turkish village of **Platáni** ❷ lies 2km (1.2 miles) southwest of Kos Town, on the road to the Asklepion, served in tourist season by a city bus from 8.10am until 10pm (last return slightly before that). Until 1971 it was commonly known as Kermédes (*Germe* in Turkish), and the Turkish community

THE LINOPÓTIS MASSACRE

Amnós tou Theoú was originally the chapel of the surrounding Catholic cemetery, containing a memorial honouring Italian officers executed by the Germans on 6 October 1943.

After Italy capitulated on 8 September 1943, Hitler ordered the shooting of captured Italian officers who assisted the British or declined to fight again for Germany. The British seized Kos on 14 September, and with the Italian garrison resisted German attacks until being overwhelmed on 3 October. Taken prisoner were 148 Italian officers; just seven opted to fight again, while 38 escaped to Turkey. The remaining 103 were marched across a field between Linopótis and the Tingáki salt-lake, supposedly towards a ship which would transport them to a POW camp. Instead they were all machine-gunned and buried where they fell.

In 1944, 66 were exhumed and re-interred in a military cemetery at Bari. Traces of the 37 others were found through a private expedition undertaken by Colonel Pietro Giovanni Luzzi during July 2015. In 1946, the German commander of Kos, General Friedrich-Wilhelm Müller, was convicted in Athens for his Cretan war crimes, and executed.

had its own primary school, but in the wake of the successive Cyprus crises and the closure of the Greek theological seminary in Istanbul, the village was officially renamed and education provided only in Greek. Subsequent emigration to Anatolia has caused Turkish numbers on Kos to drop from about 3,000 to around 700; mainly those Muslims owning real estate and businesses have stayed. Relations between them and their Greek Orthodox neighbours are cordial, and intermarriage is even beginning.

Platáni's older domestic architecture is strongly reminiscent of styles in rural Crete, from where many of the village's Muslims came between 1896 and 1912, speaking Greek rather than Turkish; Crete during that period was an autonomous region within the Ottoman Empire, but Cretan Muslims could

THE JEWS OF KOS

Jews had lived on Kos since antiquity, but the Knights of St John exiled most of this Greek-speaking community to Nice twice between 1314 and 1502. Following the Ottoman conquest, Ladino-speaking Sephardic Jews settled here, their dwindling numbers reinforced after 1922 by co-religionists from devastated İzmir in Anatolia.

Despite this long history, only two tangible traces remain of the Jewish community. On the road between Kos Town and Platáni, a Jewish cemetery lies in a dark conifer grove, 300m/yards from the main Muslim graveyard. Dates on the headstones, inscribed in both Hebrew and Italian, stop ominously in 1940. The remaining local community of about 140, together with 1,973 Rhodian Jews, was shipped to Athens in July 1944 by the Nazis, and thence to Auschwitz for extermination. Just one Koan Jew, who died early in the 1990s, survived the war. The former synagogue, back in town near the ancient agora, re-opened in 1991 as a 'municipal multipurpose hall' – it occasionally hosts concerts.

see that their island would eventually join Greece and that there would be no place for them in the new order. Kos and Rhodes were the closest, similar Ottoman-held islands to which they could flee.

At the main crossroads, with a functioning Ottoman fountain nearby, are several Muslim-owned tavernas, the main reason outsiders stop *Asklepion ruins*
here (the best are described on pages 108–09), as well as for superior ice cream at the Paradosi sweet shop.

THE ASKLEPION

The Hellenistic **Asklepion** ❸ (summer daily 8am–7.30pm, earlier closure in winter; charge), 4km (2.4 miles) south of town, is one of just three in Greece. The site was first excavated in 1902–05 by islander Iakovos Zaraftis and the German Rudolf Herzog; digging resumed under Italian archaeologists Luciano Laurenzi and Luigi Morricone.

Urban bus number 3 or a mini-train make the trip via Plátani between 8.30am and 5.30pm; otherwise you can attempt the steepish bicycle ride, perhaps pausing for lunch in Plátani en route.

The Asklepion (pronounced *asklipíon*) was actually founded just after the death of Hippocrates, but presumably the methods used and taught here were his. Both a shrine of Asklepios and a curative centre, its magnificent setting on three hillside terraces overlooking Anatolia reflects early recognition of the importance of the therapeutic environment. Two fountains provided the site with clean, fresh water – one still

Asklepios

Kos's Asklepion honours the Greek god of healing Asklepios, who according to legend was the son of Apollo and the nymph Koronis. His cult developed from the early Classical era onward, with a half-dozen combination shrines and therapy centres (the biggest at Epidauros) all over the Hellenic world.

dribbles slightly – and extensive stretches of clay piping are still visible, embedded in the ground.

Today, very little remains *above* ground, owing to periodic earthquakes and the Knights' pilfering of site masonry for their castle. The lower terrace in fact never had many structures, being instead the main venue for the *Asklepieia* – quadrennial celebrations and athletic or musical competitions in honour of the god. Sacrifices to Asklepios were conducted at an **altar**, the oldest (c. 340 BC) structure here, whose foundations lie near the middle of the second terrace. Just to its east, some Corinthian columns of a second-century AD **Roman temple** were re-erected by Laurenzini and Morricone. A monumental **staircase** flanked by *exedrae* (display niches) leads from the altar up to the second-century BC **Doric temple** of Asklepios on the topmost terrace, the last and grandest of a succession of the deity's shrines at this site, though only foundations remain.

THE NORTHEAST COAST: LÁMBI TO BROS THERMÁ

Kos Town is flanked by two areas of seafront development. **Lámbi** ❹ immediately north is essentially a suburb, albeit one devoted almost entirely to tourism, fringed by a long, east-facing beach (thus the Ottoman name Kumburnu or 'Sand Point') liberally sown with beach bars and sunbed concessions. Their biggest concentration is along Aktí Andoníou Zouroúdi, which extends almost up to Mylos, a recommended windmill beach-bar beyond the urban grid. Don't try to walk or pedal past it all the way to the end at **Cape Skandári**, as this is an off-limits military base.

The coast road southeast from town, starting at the yacht marina, curls around the northeastern tip of Kos, passing en route much of the island's luxury accommodation. **Psalídi** ❺ can be said to start at the few spiral-fluted columns of the fourth-century AD basilica of **Ágios Gavriíl**, just inland from the road in a marshy area. There are a few indifferent public beaches nearby, with sunbed-and-umbrella concessions, but most coastline here is the domain of hotels (aside from near our recommended windsurf schools beyond **Cape Loúros**).

Once past the last resort hotel on the strip – Okeanis – Ammos beach bar signals the start of an excellent, much more protected stretch of sand and pebbles extending for over 1,000m (0.6 miles) south to **Cape Ágios Fokás** ❻, with its military watchtower. While there are no facilities aside

Beaches can get really busy in the summer

from Ammos, this patch is popular with locals who come prepared with picnics and umbrellas to enjoy the clean sea here. Discreet naturism is practiced where low cliffs shield the beach from prying eyes up on the road. It's easy enough to pedal out here on a clunker bike, being only 6km (3.7 miles) from town, mostly on designated, flat cycle path.

The next decent beach is beyond the cape, between it and a final cluster of hotels. There's another beach-bar here, somewhat regimented, but the shore just east, where some tamarisks lend shade, is protected from most winds. Urban buses numbers 1 and 5 serve this route from dawn until midnight, with eight (between 10.15am–5.15pm, last return 6pm) continuing to the start of the dirt track down to Bros Thermá.

BROS AND PÍSO THERMÁ

The unusual, remote hot springs of **Bros Thermá** ❼, one of the most popular attractions on Kos, emerge from volcanic cliffs about 3km (2 miles) beyond Cape Ágios Fokás. They are most easily reached by rented vehicle (or for the very fit, multi-speed mountain-bike); the final approach lies along a dirt track heading down and left at a drinks stall just before the end of the asphalt, where buses leave you. Track roughness varies depending on the preceding winter; rent a jeep to guarantee passage. Parking is very limited and you may have to leave four-wheelers a good 300m/yards shy of the springs, certainly no further than the sunbed/snack bar concession which serves the small pebble beach at the bottom of the steep grade.

Scalding, odourless springs (45°C/113°F at source) issue from a tiny grotto at the base of the palisades, flowing through a trench to mingle with the sea at comfortable temperatures inside a giant corral of boulders. Winter storms disperse the boulder wall, re-fashioned every April, so the pool changes shape from year to year – but always has a maximum depth

Enjoying the warm waters of Bros Thermá

of about three-and-a-half feet. Despite periodic threats of development as a spa, it remains free of access, and immensely popular with tourists and locals alike, especially during the cooler months or on moonlit nights – and under a full moon, it's truly magic (provided your pool companions aren't too rowdy!).

About halfway between Bros Thermá and Kardámena, maps show another coastal hot spring at a spot marked **Píso Thermá ❽**, or Agía Iríni after the chapel there. The normally authoritative Greek-language hot-springs guide *Ta Loutra tis Ellados* claims you can walk there along the shoreline with some difficulty from Bros Thermá in two hours, as does the municipal website www.kos.gr. The Píso Thermá springs were once hotter (47°/117°F) and stronger-flowing than Bros Thermá, but during the 1970s a boulder-fall blocked their main outflow, leaving just a few warm seeps emerging from the seabed. Today people mostly go by boat from Kardámena, especially for the saint's day (May 5) pilgrimage.

Flamingos on the Alykí salt pan

NORTHWEST COAST RESORTS: TINGÁKI TO MASTIHÁRI

Scattered along the north-west-facing coast of Kos, the resorts of Tingáki, Marmári and Mastihári share an exposure to prevailing summer winds, and great Aegean views. The profiles of (west to east) Kálymnos, Psérimos and the Turkish Bodrum peninsula on the horizon make for spectacular scenery, especially at sunrise or sunset.

TINGÁKI AND MARMÁRI

Tingáki ❾ (sometimes 'Tigáki'), the shore annexe of the Asfendioú hamlets (see page 55), lies 9km (5.5miles) west of Kos Town, whether via Zipári and the main trunk road, or by more relaxing back roads preferred by cyclists. It's a busy, somewhat higgledy-piggledy resort popular with Brits, with most of its accommodation scattered inland among fields and cow pastures. The long and narrow, white-sand **beach**, fringed at the back by jujube and tamarisk trees, improves, and veers further out of earshot from the frontage road, as you head southwest from the focal seaside T-junction/plaza, with the best patches to either side of the drainage from Alykí salt lake.

Just west of the plaza, **Artemis Hamam** (daily; www.artemishamam.com), is Kos's only public, non-hotel-affiliated answer to those across the way in Bodrum. All the usual massages and therapies are available, best enjoyed in discounted packages (€50–120). There's also a shop with genuine Turkish-made hamam products plus Western lotions and oils.

The traditional coastal annexe of Pylí village, **Marmári ⑩**, 15km (9.3 miles) from Kos Town along the island trunk road, has a smaller built-up area than Tingáki; its beach is broader and arguably better, especially the section signposted as **Píthos**. To the west, the sand forms mini-dunes sheltering the odd naturist. A grid of paved rural lanes, popular with cyclists, links the inland portions of Tingáki and Marmári. Arriving along the main road, you turn off just past the little duck-pond and derelict buildings at **Linopótis**, which began life as the Italian agricultural colony Anguillara. Marmári is most popular with Germanophone and Italian visitors.

MASTIHÁRI

Although it has nearby its share of mega-all-inclusive complexes and Kos's biggest water-park, three-street-wide **Mastihári ⑫**, draped over a slope rising from the harbour, remains one of the island's more low-key resorts; it was a

---

ALYKÍ SEASONAL LAKE

Tingáki and Marmári are separated by the **Alykí salt pan ⑪**, which becomes a brackish lake lasting until next autumn after wet winters. Recent years have indeed been rainy, with flamingos (and the odd swan) arriving as early as October and staying until early June; almost 450 flamingos were counted wading over one week early in 2015. If they aren't visible here, chances are the wind has diverted them to the smaller, brackish pond near the cape at Psalídi.

Western striped-neck terrapins (*Maremys caspica rivulata*) often congregate near the seasonal lake's outlet to the sea, a sluice with a narrow road bridge over it; if they come ashore, feed them at your own risk – they have strong jaws capable of inflicting nasty wounds, or even severing fingers.

Andimáhia castle fortifications

permanent village long before tourism times, as well as the historic summer quarters of Andimáhia, 3km (1.8 miles) inland.

Mastihári, 25km (15.5 miles) from Kos Town by the most direct route, is also the **ferry port** for the shortest crossing to Kálymnos; most of the year there are morning, mid-afternoon and early evening ro-ro sailings (Wed and Sun no midday sailing), keyed more or less to the arrival times of flights from Athens – KTEL buses to or from Kos Town make a stop in Mastihári en route, dovetailing with the comings and goings of the ferry.

While shorter than those at Marmári or Tingáki, the local **beach** extending to the southwest is broader, with dunes (and no sunbeds) towards the far end. The early sixth-century basilica of **Ágios Ioánnis** ⓯ (fenced but unlocked) lies about 1.5km (1 mile) down this beach, following the shoreline promenade (look for the enclosure near the Hotel Ahilleos). The basilica is fairly typical of the island's numerous early Christian monuments, with a row of column bases separating a pair of side aisles from the nave, a tripartite narthex and a baptistry tacked onto the north side of the building. It was excavated during the 1950s by the great Byzantinologist and architect Anastasios Orlandos, but regrettably its intricate floor mosaics are covered in protective gravel.

ANDIMÁHIA, KARDÁMENA AND PLÁKA

Visitors inevitably pass through blufftop **Andimáhia** ⓮, immediately northeast of the airport, but few stop in the village itself as there are no conventional attractions aside from an old restored windmill, kitted out as a museum with sails rigged (though not turning). This is the last surviving mill of more than thirty which once dotted the ridges here and at Kéfalos. You can inspect the inner workings (daily 9am–5.30pm; charge).

More compelling is **Andimáhia castle** ⓯, about 4km (2.4 miles) southeast of the village, mostly by a diffidently signposted if paved side-road beginning at an army camp. Enormous when seen from afar, this triangular stronghold of the Knights Hospitaller overlooks Nísyros and Tílos, and would have been a vital signalling link between those islands and the Knights' castle at present-day Bodrum in Turkey. The originally Byzantine castle was initially used by the Knights as a prison, then modified during the 1490s in tandem with improved fortifications at Kos port citadel.

The fortifications (unrestricted entry) prove less intimidating close up – except for a rather pathetic old man, dressed in mainland evzone costume the likes of which has never been worn on Kos, who accosts all visitors with a loud, barked 'Tradizionale!' and demands money to be photographed. A less authentic or edifying spectacle cannot be imagined; nearby villagers are embarrassed by him but, since he is breaking no law, there is nothing to be done about it.

Once past the fake evzone and through the imposing double north gateway, surmounted by the arms of Grand Master Pierre d'Aubusson dated 1494, you can follow the well-preserved west parapet. The badly crumbled eastern wall presides over a sharp drop to ravines draining towards Kardámena. Inside the walls stand **two chapels**: the

The taverna scene in Kardámena

westerly, dedicated to Ágios Nikólaos, retains a fresco of Ágios Hristóforos (St Christopher) carrying the Christ Child, while the eastern one of Agía Paraskeví, though mostly devoid of wall painting, sports fine rib vaulting springing from half-columns. Gravel walkways, illumination and a ticket booth were installed in 2001 – and never really used except when there's a summer concert here, arguably the best time to visit.

KARDÁMENA

Some 5km (3 miles) southeast of the airport, **Kardámena** ⑯ is the closest resort to it, just pipping Mastihári, and the largest (1,650) coastal settlement outside of Kos Town. Good, though not uninterrupted, beaches stretching to either side, plus a seafront promenade and *platía* with a few minor Italian-era buildings, are the sum of its daytime charms. After dark there's a lively bar and club scene, though nothing like Kardámena's 1990s heyday as designated party resort for younger Brits. There's a broader profile of visitors lately – especially Russians, young couples and families – and bars with naughty or Brit-centric names like 'Ten Toes Up, Ten Toes Down' or 'Slug and Lettuce' are now rare if not completely extinct.

Northeast of the resort centre, the best patch of **beach** from the standpoint of amenities, no-hassle parking, good sand and access to exceptionally clean sea free of reef or sharp-edged pebbles is in front of Atlantis Taverna, about 1.5km (1 mile) out of town, which rents sunbeds and parasols affordably.

Beaches southwest of Kardámena tend to be scrappier and monopolised by mega-hotels. It is possible to drive back to the main road directly along here without retracing your steps via the airport, but between the Lakitra and Robinson Club resorts, a stretch of rough, steep dirt road is best tackled with a jeep, especially after hard winters.

PLÁKA FOREST

Just west of the airport on the main island trunk road, signs indicate an initially paved turning to 'Pláka'. The road soon becomes dirt (but always passable) as one descends into the densely forested **Pláka** ⑰ dell. The main attraction here, besides welcome shade, is a thriving population (c. 30) of wild but camera-friendly peacocks – shrieking, flying up into the trees and marching lines of their offspring around. Local feral cats have learned, presumably after some well-aimed pecks from the parents, to leave the chicks alone. It's a great outing for kids, as the peafowl are not otherwise aggressive.

SOUTH-COAST BEACHES: POLÉMI TO KÉFALOS

Climbing out of Pláka valley back up onto the main island road, and then heading southwest, drivers soon see profuse signage pointing left (south) and down – sometimes sharply down – to the best beaches on Kos. This is essentially one giant, 5km- (3-miles) strip of sand up to Cape Tigáni, but subdivided into separate patches with individual access roads, whose Greek and touristic-English names co-exist on placards. Beyond Ágios Stéfanos and Kastrí islet, Kéfalos Bay extends along another 3.5km (2.2 miles) of sandy beach.

The beach sections, described below from east to west, are all provided with sunbeds, a rudimentary snack/drinks-bar and often a jet-ski franchise. **Magic** ⑱, officially Polémi, is the longest, broadest and wildest section, with a full-service taverna above the car park (see page 109), no jet skis and a nudist zone (**Exotic**) at the east end. **Sunny**, officially signed as Psilós Gremós and easily walkable from Magic, has another taverna and jet-skis. **Langádes (Markos)** ⑲ is the cleanest and most picturesque section of beach, with junipers tumbling off the dunes almost to the shore. **Paradise**, alias Bubble Beach in boat-trip jargon owing to volcanic gas vents in the shallows, is overrated; the sandy area is too small for the crowds descending upon its wall-to-wall sunbeds and tavernas, while boats attached to paragliding and banana-ride outfits, plus the inevitable jet-skis, buzz constantly offshore. **Camel** (Kamíla) ⑳ is the shortest and loneliest of these strands, flanked by weird rock formations (but no humped beasts) and protected somewhat from crowds by the very steep, unpaved drive in past its hillside taverna; the shore here is fine sand, with no jet skis and good snorkelling on either side of the cove.

Uninterrupted sand resumes at **Ágios Stéfanos** ㉑ peninsula, with beaches to either side; the left-hand (easterly) one, with sunbeds, is backed by a now-abandoned Club Med complex. The sparsely marked public access road to Ágios Stéfanos begins near a bus stop on the highway, cutting through the Club Med grounds. Two triple-aisled, late-fifth-to-early sixth-century **basilicas** occupy the peninsula. Once the premier early-Christian monuments on Kos, they are now in disgraceful condition. All of the columns have been toppled by vandals since the 1980s, and the rich mosaics which cover the entire floor have either been damaged or covered in a thick layer of protective sand. You'll need a plastic beach trowel or a thick brush to uncover two peacocks perching upon and drinking from a goblet, or (in the north basilica, next to the baptistry) two ducks paddling about. All that said, Ágios Stéfanos is still the best pre-served such complex on the island, and a wonderfully atmospheric spot.

The Ágios Stéfanos ruins overlook Kastrí islet

The basilicas overlook tiny, striking **Kastrí** islet, sport-ing a chapel and a distinct volcanic pinnacle. From the sandy cove west of the peninsula it's just a short swim away; in spots, you can even wade. The shallow sea here warms up early in the year and stays that way into November, offering the best snorkelling on an island not otherwise known for it, owing to rock formations cutting across the generally sandy seabed. As at Paradise beach, gas bubbles up from the ocean floor.

The main road southwest from here runs behind a service-able but not spectacular beach, of equal interest to windsurf-ers and bathers. Resort development here is modest, formerly pitched at budget-conscious Brits a generation or so older than at Kardámena, but clientele is now more mixed, including many Russians. The strip of scattered one- or two-star hotels, low-rise apartments, tavernas and bars ends at **Kamári ㉒**, the far end of the bay and the fishing-port annexe of Kéfalos village overhead. Boat trips may be offered out of Kamári, but probably no further than Bubble Beach and certainly not to Nísyros.

KÉFALOS – THE WILD WEST

The extreme southwestern tip of Kos, a sparsely inhabited monster-head-shaped landmass, is a semi-mythical paradise for island foodies – literally a land of milk and honey, source of the best island cheese, honey and bread. There is just one inland village, **Kéfalos ㉓**, 43km (26.5miles) from the capital and the terminus for buses. Squatting on a flat-topped hill, looking northeast along the length of Kos, Kéfalos has little to recommend it other than a single ATM and a few basic snack bars. Even the **Knights' castle** here, downhill beside the Kamári road, is rudimentary – hardly more than a signalling tower – and

Remote Kávo Paradíso beach

unimpressive; the Knights abandoned it in 1504. But the village makes a natural staging point for expeditions south into the rugged peninsula that terminates at sheer Cape Kríkello.

THE KÉFALOS PENINSULA

The first point of interest is Byzantine **Panagía Palatianí**, 1km (0.6 miles) south of Kéfalos; a signposted dirt track (passable to ordinary cars) east from the roadside leads to a parking area by a modern church. Just below stands the fenced-off 9th- or 10th-century chapel, built entirely from masonry of an ancient temple.

Some 500m/yards beyond, there's contrastingly no signage for ancient **Astypalaia** ㉔, the original capital of Kos until abandoned in 366 BC. Your clue is the large, roadside parking area with a dry fountain, opposite an unlocked gate. It's a two-minute path-walk down to a late Classical **amphitheatre** with two rows of seats still in place, enjoying a fine prospect over the curve of Kéfalos Bay – a lovely, pine-shaded spot despite the scanty remains of this once-important city.

Immediately past Astypalaia, a paved side-road leaves the ridge road and heads west towards **Ágios Theológos** ㉕ beach, 6km (3.7 miles) from Kéfalos. Besides the saint's chapel, there's an eponymous taverna which takes full advantage of its local monopoly – just stop in for dessert and a drink perhaps. Forays along the dirt tracks to either side – a jeep or dirt-bike is advisable – will reveal secluded sandy coves below low cliffs.

Appealing **Ágios Ioánnis Thymianós monastery** ㉖ (6.5km/ 4 miles from Kéfalos), reached by following the paved road to its end, is almost the end of the line for non-4WD vehicles (jeeps can reach Ágios Mámas, 4.5km/2.8 miles beyond, almost at the cape). Set on a natural balcony under two plane trees, the church is locked except during the festival on 28–29 August; it's a fine picnic spot at other times.

Pylí castle overlooks old village ruins

The dirt track heading straight south beyond the monastery goes 1.8km (1.1 miles) to a crossroads; turn hard right here and head another 2km (1.2 miles) down to the island's remotest beach, **Kávo Paradíso** ㉗ (officially **Halandríou**). Jeep drivers will feel more confident – after a harsh winter one could ground a saloon car in the deep ruts along the last kilometre, though with extra care plenty of small cars make it through. Kávo Paradíso, a vast expanse of sand and clean (if often surfy) sea with a dramatic mountain for a backdrop, is worth the effort; clothing is optional and most years a snack bar with sunbeds operates June–Sept.

The only other notable beaches around Kéfalos are up on its north shore. **Limniónas** ㉘ (sometimes Limiónas) is 4km (2.4 miles) due north of the village by good road; there are actually two protected sandy coves here (one with sunbeds), separated by an isthmus leading to the little fishing anchorage. **Kohylári**, further east along the same coast, is too exposed to interest folk other than kitesurfers; see page 85 for details.

AROUND MT DÍKEOS

The main interest of inland Kos resides in the hamlets on the north slope of **Mount Díkeos** (the ancient Oromedon). This cluster of settlements, collectively called **Asfendioú**, nestles amid the island's only natural forest and provides a glimpse of what Kos looked like before tourism and concrete took hold. They can be reached from the island trunk road via the extremely curvy side road from Zipári, 7.5km (4.6 miles) from Kos Town; a minimally signposted but paved, straighter minor road to Lagoúdi starting about 1km (0.6 miles) further west; or the shorter access road to Pylí from Linopótis pond.

PYLÍ: NEW AND OLD

Just over 13km (8 miles) from Kos Town along the main highway, **Linopótis** is a sunken, spring-fed pond, alive with ducks and eels. From the junction here, a good road leads southeast to contemporary **Pylí** ㉙, which divides into two districts. In the upper neighbourhood, 150m/yards west of the main square and church, Pigí district comprises a lush oasis with a recommended taverna (see page 110) and a giant, sixteenth-century cistern-fountain, the *pigí* of the name, with four lion-head spouts – the water is excellent and constantly collected by locals.

Pylí's other monument is the so-called **Harmýlio** (Tomb of Harmylos), signposted near the top of the village en route to Kardámena as 'Heroön of Charmylos', a mythical ancient king of Kos. This consists of a subterranean vault (fenced off) with twelve niches, probably a Hellenistic family tomb. Immediately above it, ample masonry of an ancient temple, perhaps dedicated to demigod Harmylos, has been incorporated into the medieval **chapel of Stavrós**.

PALEÓ PYLÍ

Paleó (old) **Pylí** ㉚, just under 3km (2 miles) southeast of its modern descendant, was the Byzantine capital of Kos, inhabited from about the tenth century until the Ottoman conquest. Head there via Amanioú, keeping straight at the junction where signs point left to Ziá and Lagoúdi. The road continues up to a wooded canyon, dwindling to a dirt track beside a trough-spring for local livestock. Some five minutes' walk uphill from the spring along the track are the remains of a **water mill** in the ravine just west.

From opposite the trough, a stair-path leads within fifteen minutes to an 11th-century **Byzantine castle**, whose partly intact roof affords superb views. En route you pass the ruins of the abandoned village, as well as three fourteenth- or fifteenth-century **churches**. That of **Arhángelos**, the first encountered, retains substantial fourteenth-century frescoes, particularly numerous scenes from the life of Christ on the vaulted ceiling, including a fine *Betrayal* in the north vault. Unfortunately it is usually locked following 2012 restoration, but should it be open, make it a priority to pop inside. Outside are the remains of a graceful Latin arcade of a type usually only seen on Rhodes or Cyprus. Rectangular **Ágios Nikólaos**

Ziá is the place to be at sunset

(unlocked), just south of the route to the citadel, has a *Communion of the Apostles* in the apse, while **Ypapandí**, the largest church and nearest the castle, is almost bare inside but impresses with its barrel vaulting supported by re-used ancient columns.

LAGOÚDI

From Paleó Pylí, return to the junction in Amanioú and turn right (east) through **Konidário**, an abandoned Muslim village that's now a forest reserve and picnic grounds. After 3km (2 miles) you reach picturesque **Lagoúdi ③**, with the prominent **Génnisis Theotókou church** at the village summit. Its interior shelters vivid 1980s frescoes by reclusive iconographer Nikos Vlahogiannis. If he's still living adjacent, friendly Father Kyriakos will greet you.

> ### Mt Díkeos the Just
>
> 'Díkeos' means just or righteous in Greek, and local legend asserts that the mountain assumed this demotic name (versus the ancient Oromedon) because it is 'just' in directing its abundant waters to flow usefully north to the island's villages and fields, rather than pointlessly south into the sea.

EVANGELÍSTRIA AND ZÍA

The first Asfendioú village encountered, either heading east from Lagoúdi or going up the curvy side-road from Zipári, is **Evangelístria ②**. Beyond the eponymous parish church extends a neighbourhood of low, whitewashed houses, now mostly abandoned following the stampede down to the coast; the remainder have been bought up and restored by outsiders.

Further up the twisty road from Evangelístria, **Ziá**'s **③** spectacular views and sunsets make it the hapless target of numerous tour buses each evening. Just six people still dwell full-time in the village, but otherwise any building on the main street that isn't a taverna is a souvenir shop. The only sight is the preserved water-mill on the grounds of the recommended Neromylos Café (see page 109).

ASCENT OF HRISTÓS PEAK

Ziá is the classic trailhead for the ascent of 840-metre (2730ft-) high **Hristós peak ㉞**, by a paltry three metres (10 ft) the second highest point of the Díkeos range. Taking rather less than half a day, this is within the capabilities of any reasonably fit, properly shod person, and offers arguably the best views in the Dodecanese. Except on the date (6 August) of the annual pilgrimage climb, you will see few or no other hikers.

At Ziá's upper Platía Karydiás, with its fig tree in a round masoned enclosure and Neromylos Café, find the step-path indicated as 'Dikaios Mountain Kefalovrisi'. Some five minutes up this, you'll pass the seldom-open Kefalovrisi Taverna, and then onto a dirt track for a few minutes more to **Isódia tís Theotókou** chapel with its vaulted roof, covered porch and bomb nose-cone hung as the bell. Bear right at the junction behind it – blue arrows guide you, and the surface underfoot is briefly cemented – and head west past Ziá's last house.

Some fifteen minutes from Platía Karydiás, you pass **Ágios Geórgios** chapel, locked to protect its frescoes (some visible through the door window). The rough onward track, just passable to vehicles, curls gradually south past one large and one small rural cottage; beyond Ágios Geórgios, a section of path marked by cairns shortcuts a wide bend in the track (though takes time to get through a wire-fastened gate across the path).

Thirty-five minutes above Platía Karydiás, you'll reach the true trailhead amidst a juniper grove. The spot is fairly obvious; boulders flanking the path have blue paint dots and the word 'Dikeos'. There's also a triangular metal sign in Greek Byzantine script ('Χριστός') and just uphill stone cairns and more paint marks.

Mountainous landscape south of Ziá

The distinct trail zigzags eastwards up the mountainside, leaving the junipers within twenty minutes and arriving just over an hour out of Ziá at the ridge leading northeast to the summit. The grade slackens, and several shattered cisterns, once used by shepherds, are seen north of the path.

From the moment the ridge is attained, it's another twenty minutes maximum to the peak along the watershed, usually just to its north. The little pillbox-like chapel of **Metamórfosi tou Sotírou**, visible most of the time, stands about 40m/yards northeast of the altitude survey marker; there's also a small bad-weather shelter nearby, possibly a roofed-over cistern. Just north of this, you can ponder the esoteric symbolism of a giant crucifix fashioned from PVC sewer pipes and filled with concrete.

Turkey's Knidos Peninsula dominates the **view** to the southeast; Nísyros, Tílos and Hálki float to the south; Astypálea closes off the horizon on the west; Kálymnos and, on a good day, Léros, are spread out to the north; and the entire west and north portions of Kos are laid out before you.

The south flank of Mt Díkeos takes a steep dive towards the Aegean; those intent on visiting remote Theológos chapel down this slope should engage a qualified local guide. The ridge continuing northeast to the true summit (843m/2740ft) can only be tackled by technical climbers – there are too many knife-edge saddles and arêtes. So the sole feasible descent involves retracing your steps, which takes just ten minutes less than the climb, owing to the rough surface. Allow two hours thirty minutes minimum walking time for the out-and-back trip from Ziá – three-plus hours inclusive of photo and rest stops.

On the ferry

ASÓMATOS AND HAÏHOÚTES

The paved road east of Ziá threads through the densest forest on Mt Díkeos – mixed juniper and pine – and also passes two of the more interesting Asfendioú hamlets. **Asómatos**, with views rivalling Ziá's (but no amenities), is still home to perhaps thirty villagers plus a handful of foreigners and Athenians renovating houses. The place really only comes to life at the November 7–8 festival of the gaily painted central **Arhángelos church**, whose spacious courtyard (usually locked) features a fine pebble mosaic.

Haïhoútes ㉟, officially Ágios Dimítrios but increasingly referred to by its Ottoman name, lies 2km (1.2 miles) further. It was abandoned entirely during 1967–74, when the villagers departed for Zipári or further afield. Today, there are signs of revival, with eight residents, old-house renovations and a pleasant café operating just uphill from the reliable, potable fountain. In the narthex of the attractive central **church**, a small photo display documents a considerable population during the 1940s, when the village was a centre of resistance against the occupation.

The road continues another 6km (3.7 miles) to the Asklepion, completing your circuit of the island.

EXCURSIONS

Kos offers opportunities to visit several Dodecanesian neighbours on separate day-trips, or overnight stays. Catamarans make it possible to design your own itineraries without signing on to organised excursions available from boats moored at Mandráki port.

Closest is volcanic Nísyros on the south, with its caldera and photogenic villages. Northwest lies craggy Kálymnos, once a sponge-divers' island, and its sleepy satellite islets Psérimos and Télendos, ideal day-trip destinations from Kálymnos. Beyond Kálymnos, Léros merits a visit for a fine castle and 1930s Streamline Modern architecture. Last and remotest, the holy island of Pátmos beckons with its fortified summit monastery and the enchanting surrounding village. You can also pop over to Bodrum in Turkey, whose lights are clearly visible by night northeast of Kos.

NÍSYROS

In legend Poseidon, battling the titan Polybotes, tore a rock from Kos and crushed his adversary beneath it. The rock

The blue balconies and white houses of Mandráki

became **Nísyros** ㊱. Hardly less prosaic are the facts of a prehistoric eruption, when this volcano-island apparently blew its top Krakatoa-style. Notably fertile despite lacking water, Nísyros has proven attractive and wealthy enough to keep almost 1,000 permanent inhabitants (down, though, from 5,000 in 1912, and 2,600 in 1947). While remittances from overseas (particularly New York) are vital, most income is derived from offshore **Gyalí** islet, a vast lump of pumice and perlite slowly being quarried by a score of miners. Rent collected by the municipality from the mining concession funds a public bakery, pharmacy and well-padded civil service. Accordingly, islanders bother little with agriculture besides keeping cows; hillside terraces meticulously fashioned for grain and grapes lie abandoned, and winemaking has ceased.

Day-trips from either Kardámena or Kos Town typically arrive at 10.30–11am, with passengers whisked immediately by coach up to the volcanic caldera in the interior before transfer back downhill for lunch and departure at 3.30–4pm. But visiting just for the day is a pity, as Nísyros fully deserves an overnight or two. Hire a scooter or car from Manos K (tel: 22420 31029) on the port, or trust public buses and your own feet.

Away from its harbour, **Mandráki** ⏺ proves an attractive, deceptively large capital, with blue patches of sea visible (and audible) at the end of narrow, cat-thronged streets. Brightly painted wooden balconies and shutters hang cheerfully from tall, white houses ranged around a central communal orchard. The well-labelled **archaeological museum** (Tue–Sun 8.30am–2.40pm; charge) does a gallop, over two floors, through local history, from Archaic grave goods to Roman stelae and Byzantine painted bowls. Overhead, a **Knights' castle** (best appreciated from Hohláki beach behind) shelters the earlier **Panagía Spilianí monastery** with its grotto-like church, built in accordance with instructions from the Virgin herself, who appeared in a vision to an islander. On the way up, the local **folklore museum** (unreliable hours May–Sept; charge), with traditional paraphernalia and archival photos, is worth a glance if open. During 1996–97, the Langadáki district just below was rocked by multiple earthquakes, damaging numerous houses (mostly repaired).

As a defensive bastion, the seventh-century-BC Doric **Paleó-kastro** (unrestricted access), a short walk out of Langadáki, is far more impressive than the Knights' castle, and one of the finest ancient forts in Greece. You can clamber up onto massive, polygonal-block walls, standing to their original height, using a broad staircase inside the still-intact gateway.

THE VOLCANIC ZONE

As you approach the **Lakkí volcanic zone** ⏺ (12.5km/8miles from Mandráki), a rotten-egg stench greets you as vegetation gradually yields to lifeless, caked powder. The sunken main crater, **Stéfanos**, is an extraordinary moonscape of grey, brown and jaundice-yellow 260 metres (845ft) across; another, less visited double crater (dubbed **Polyvótis**), even more dramatic, awaits to the west, created between 1873 and 1888. Steam-puffing fumaroles in the craters accumulate little pincushions of sulphur crystals.

Standing on the floor of Stéfanos (stick to trodden areas, the crust is thin elsewhere) you hear mud boiling away below you – the groaning of trapped Polybotes, for some 45,000 years according to geologists. The most recent eruptions, which produced steam, ash and earthquakes, occurred in 1422, 1873, 1888 and 1933 – the volcano is merely dormant. The Greek power corporation made exploratory geothermal soundings nearby until 1993, when it departed, stymied by islander hostility – though not before destroying the 1,000-year-old cobbled road down to Mandráki.

Four eucalypts shade a drinks kantína in the centre of the wasteland; a ticket booth flanking the access road charges admission to the area in season. The easiest path up to Polyvótis begins along the fence 20m/yards beyond the kantína.

VILLAGES AND WALKS

Two photogenic villages perch above Lakkí. Nearly abandoned **Emboriós** (pop. 27), with a tiny summit castle, is slowly being bought up and restored by outsiders, who often discover natural saunas in the basements of their crumbling houses; at the village outskirts there's a signposted public **sauna** the grotto entrance outlined in white paint. (Most Emboriots relocated to the fishing/yacht port of Pálli after World War II.)

Nikiá ③⑨, 13km (8 miles) from Mandráki's port, is busier, with 61 registered inhabitants and there are also signs of renovation activity. The quirky round *platía* has one café and you can visit the moderately worthwhile **Museum of Vulcanology**, occupying the disused school (Mon–Thu 11.30am–6.30pm, Fri–Sat 10.30am–2.30pm; charge). For most visitors though, the unlocked cemetery chapel of **Agía Triáda**, with its 15th-century frescoes, will prove more tempting.

Nísyros offers good **walks** through countryside green with oak or terebinth, on a network of fitfully marked and maintained trails; these are traced correctly on the recommended map. Autumn is a wonderful time, especially for the succulent local figs (the Turks called the island *İncirli*, 'Fig Place').

Walking on Stéfanos crater is an exhilarating experience

You can sample the best routes in a single day, by starting with a mid-morning bus ride to Nikiá. From beside the museum, follow a sign downhill, then right, towards eyrie-like **Ágios Ioánnis Theológos monastery**, then continue north 90min towards Emboriós (there's 1.3km/0.8 miles of unavoidable road-slogging). After lunch there, head west, starting near the little castle, for 45min to **Evangelístria monastery**, a major hikers' junction. Allow time for a detour (2hr return) up the well-marked path to island summit **Profítis Ilías** (698m/2268ft), with a chapel and views to rival those from Hristós on Kos. From Evangelístria, complete a long but satisfying itinerary by descending 40min to Mandráki, via little 18th-century **Armás church**, with vivid frescoes, the best easily accessible ones on Nísyros.

Póthia's town hall

BEACHES AND BATHS

Hohláki, reached by masoned pathway, lies 10min beyond Mandráki – a prime sunset-watching venue, but the sea can be choppy and the coarse pebbles aren't very comfortable. The sandy beach extending east from **Pálli** is more user-friendly, with a few tamarisks for shade. Halfway between Mandráki and Pálli, the **Dimotiká Loutrá** (Public Baths) were refurbished in 2015 with quality marble tubs (unpredictable hours; 20-min soak for a charge). Upstairs is a basic inn, and at the corner of the building a sympathetic if pricey ouzerí. The only other **thermal pool** on Nísyros is in front of Mandráki's Haritos Hotel (€5 charge for non-guests).

Nísyros's longest, best, cleanest and least windy beaches lie on the east coast, 9km/5.5miles from Mandráki. Sandy **Liés** marks the end of the road, with a summer (late June–early Sept) snack bar and parking area. From there a 15-minute trail past volcanic-ash cliffs leads to **Pahiá Ámmos** ④⓪ (Fat Sand), exactly that – 300m/yards of grey-pink stuff heaped into dunes behind, limited shade at the far end, and a constituency of naturists and free campers.

KÁLYMNOS

First impressions of **Kálymnos** ④, northwest of Kos, are of an arid, mountainous landmass with a decidedly masculine energy in the main port town of Póthia. The former dominant industry, sponge-diving, has now been supplanted by tourism and commercial fishing. But the island's prior mainstay is evident in home decor of huge sponges or shell-encrusted amphorae, and souvenir shops overflowing with smaller sponges.

Kálymnos essentially consists of two cultivated, inhabited valleys sandwiched between three limestone ridges, harsh in the full glare of noon but magically tinted towards dusk. The climate, especially in winter, is alleged to be drier and healthier than on its neighbours, since the quick-draining limestone strata, riddled with many caves, doesn't retain much moisture. Kálymnos's position and excellent harbours ensure that it has always been important – especially during Byzantine rule, which left many ruined basilicas here. Another Byzantine legacy is the survival of peculiar medieval names (Skévos, Sakellários and Mikés for men, Themélina, Petránda and Sevastí for women), found nowhere else in Greece.

PÓTHIA AND AROUND

Póthia ④ itself (population 12,324), the third-largest town in the Dodecanese, is noisy and workaday Greek, its brightly painted houses rising in tiers up the flanking hillsides. Mansions and vernacular dwellings with ornate balconies and wrought-iron ornamentation (an island speciality) are particularly evident in Evangelístria district. Florestano di Fausto's 1926–28 administration building and Rodolfo Petracco's

Hrysoheriás castle fresco

1934 town hall and market complex bracketing Hristós church deserve a look.

The most dazzling conventional attraction is the **Archaeological Museum** (Apr–Nov Tue–Sat 9am–4pm; charge). Stars of the displays include a huge Hellenistic cult statue of Asklepios; an unusual robed, child-sized *kouros* (most were naked); and a life-size third- or second-century BC bronze of a clad woman with her right hand raised in admonition, retrieved by fishermen in 1994 and inevitably dubbed '**The Lady of Kálymnos**'.

The **Nautical and Folklore Museum** (Mon–Fri 10am–1.30pm; charge for Folklore section), on the seaward side of Hristós cathedral, contains fascinating photos of old Póthia (no quay, jetty, roads, or sumptuous mansions in the 1880s) and equipment from seafarers' lives, including ingenious, dart-shaped nautical-mile logs, dragged off the stern; dangerously primitive divers' breathing apparati; and wicker 'cages' to keep propellers from cutting air lines, a constant hazard.

Northwest of Póthia loom two **castles** (daily all day; free): **Hrysoheriás**, the Knights Hospitaller stronghold adapted from a prior Byzantine fort, where the views appeal more than anything inside, and the purely Byzantine castle of **Péra Kástro** above Horió, still Kálymnos' second town. Although this pirate-proof citadel was inhabited until the late 1700s, there are few standing structures inside besides several unlocked churches offering fragmentary 15th- or 16th-century frescoes.

West from Horió, some 200m/yards past the airport road, stand the two most intact, and easiest found, of Kálymnos' Byzantine basilicas. Whitewashed steps lead over a stone wall to **Hristós tis Ierousalím (Limniótissa) basilica**, supposedly built by Byzantine Emperor Arkadios (395–408 AD) in gratitude for deliverance from a storm, though sixth-century construction is far more likely. The ornate apse with bishops' throne is fully preserved, as are sections of marble flooring; both incorporate inscribed masonry taken from a Hellenistic Apollo temple nearby. One field east, reached by a separate path from the road, is larger, three-aisled but less impressive **Agía Sofía basilica**; again the apse is the best preserved bit, used as a chapel after the rest of the complex was destroyed during 7th-century Arab raids.

VATHÝS AND BEYOND

The main sight northeast of Póthia is **Vathýs ㊸**, the island's main oasis, 11km/miles away by road. The first stretch is grimly industrial, passing a boatyard, a power plant, tank farms, quarries and a rubbish tip. None of this prepares you for a sudden road-bend and dramatic view to Vathýs far below, its green contrasting sharply with the mineral grey and orange uphill. This long, fertile valley, carpeted with walled orange and tangerine groves threaded by a maze of lanes, seems a continuation of cobalt-blue Rína fjord penetrating the landscape here. **Rína** itself is popular with yachties and accordingly has a clutch of overpriced tavernas at the head of the port, but no beach.

Without a vehicle, the best (and a popular) way to reach Vathýs is by **hiking** along the old **cobbled trail** from beside Agía

Triáda church in Póthia's Evangelístria district, arrowed conspicuously on a wall as 'Italian path'. It takes an hour to reach the pass (400m/1,312 ft elevation) in the ridge overhead, and another forty minutes downhill to Plátanos hamlet in the oasis.

Once at Plátanos, collect water from the potable spring under the namesake plane tree and ponder a continuation. You can loop back to **Horió** on a major trail around the shoulder of Profítis Ilías (676m/yards), descending a scenic gorge, or carry on from Metóhi hamlet with its frescoed Taxiárhis chapel to the start of the two-hour path to Arginónda (with some brief road-walking in the middle). Have lunch and a swim in coastal **Arginónda**, then catch a bus back to town – you may have to road-walk 5km (3 miles) to Armeós to get one. All these routes are detailed accurately on the recommended Anavasi map.

Télendos, as seen here from Kálymnos heights, is popular with rock-climbers – and it is clear why

BROSTÁ: THE WEST COAST

The string of **beach resorts** on the west coast are referred to collectively as 'Brostá' (Forward), the leading side of Kálymnos, as opposed to 'Píso' (Behind), the Póthia area.

Kandoúni ④ attracts mostly Greek and local clientele, the latter owning summer villas here; the beach – 200m/yards of brown, hard-packed sand – isn't brilliant. Especially towards sunset, take the obvious coastal path southwest to the little monastery of **Ágios Fótis** (80min return hike), offering seascapes, cliffs and a ravine.

Snail or princess?

Legend asserts that the mountainous bulk of Télendos, viewed at dusk from Kálymnos, is the petrified reclining head of a princess, gazing out to sea following her unhappy affair with the mythical prince of nearby ancient Kastélli. The less romantically inclined will only see the silhouette of a snail.

Smaller **Linária** cove, just north of Kandoúni bay, has better sand, tavernas and cafés, plus separate road access. Walk around the corner (or again distinct vehicle access) to **Platýs Gialós** beach, opposite Agía Kyriakí islet, with Kálymnos's best sand; a pity the sea is often turbid.

The main road, descending in zigzags, meets the sea again 8km (5 miles) from Póthia at **Melitsáhas** and **Myrtiés** ④, which share Kálymnos' much-diminished beach-tourism trade with **Masoúri** and **Armeós**, just north but reached by an upper bypass road, part of a circular one-way system. Melitsáhas and Myrtiés have the best beaches and cleanest sea, but these contiguous resorts have partly reinvented themselves to host spring and autumn rock-climbers.

Beyond Armeós, the road mostly hugs the coast en route to **Emboriós** ④, end of the line 20km (12 miles) from Póthia. This has average tavernas, a mixed bag of beaches to either side (some only path-accessible) and late-afternoon taxi-boat service back to Myrtiés. Buses beyond Armeós are rare, but Kálymnos is ideally explorable by scooter; the only rental outlet in Póthia is Auto Market near Ágios Nikólaos church (tel: 22430 24202, www.kalymnoscars.gr).

TÉLENDOS

These resorts' most appealing feature is the striking islet of **Télendos** ⑰ opposite, which frames some of the Aegean's more dramatic sunsets. Home to 45 winter inhabitants, Télendos is car-free and tranquil, though tourism (including rock-climbing) has certainly arrived, via little taxi-boats crossing the straits

Grafiótissa beach, Psérimos

from Myrtiés jetty (daily half-hourly 8am–11pm). Télendos was sundered from Kálymnos by the cataclysmic 554 AD earthquake; remains of a submerged town lurk at the bottom of the channel.

The single waterside hamlet huddles under **Mount Ráhi** (459 metres/1,492ft). Halfway up the north side of the mountain, an hour's trek away by paint-marked path, perches the fortified chapel of **Ágios Konstandínos**, with excellent views. Less energetic souls explore the ruined Byzantine basilicas of **Ágios Vassílios** and **Agía Tríada** at the northern and western edges of the hamlet.

Beaches vary in consistency and size; a long, sandy, tamarisk-shaded one stretches north of 'town', while scenic **Hohlakás**, 10 minutes west, has coin-sized pebbles (and sunbeds) on two separate bays, as do three smaller coves beyond the sand beach, with usually clean water: **Pláka**, **Pótha** and **Paradise** (naturist, 20min away).

PSÉRIMOS

Kálymnos' other satellite islet, **Psérimos** ❹❽ (permanent population 35), is an idyllic place once the daily crop of trippers leaves sandy Avlákia bay, with only cicadas in the huge communal olive grove to break the stillness. Excursion boats from Kos operate 'three-island' tours (€25–30) which spend just one hour at Psérimos before pushing on to nearby **Pláti** islet (1 chapel, 1 villa) for more swimming before a rushed lunch on Kálymnos. We don't recommend these tours, and the only way to spend a whole day on Psérimos – well worth it – is to depart from Kálymnos daily at 9.30am on the little ro-ro ferry Maniaï, returning at 5pm (€10; 55min journey each way). The islanders themselves use this boat for shopping and administrative business; there is only a primary school on Psérimos. During summer, one speedboat per day also calls from Mastihári on Kos.

West-facing **Avlákia**, the port and only village (including several tavernas), is fronted by a magnificent sandy beach where most trippers park themselves. For those with six hours to spend on Psérimos, there are two other, remoter beaches: clean **Vathý** (sand and gravel), a well-marked, thirty-minute path-walk east of Avlákia, or idyllic all-sand **Grafiótissa** beach to the northwest.

The path there starts from the northwestern-most house in Avlákia; go anticlockwise around its perimeter fence to see a light-green paint arrow pointing right towards an obvious

The Italian legacy in Lakkí

trail, which passes between a prominent tree and a concrete survey marker, over a low ridge. The way becomes increasingly obvious, with more green- or white-painted arrows, dashes and blobs to dispel doubt. Allow just over half an hour to reach the ruined old church of **Panagía Grafiótissa** (festival Aug 14–15), chopped in two by the sea, with just the apsidal half clinging to the low cliff. Nobody alive today on Psérimos can remember a time when it was intact. The modern replacement church just inland has a rain cistern with a bucket for water emergencies. The beach below – a vast expanse of blonde sand lapped by sea of a near-Caribbean hue – is the whole point. There's some reef offshore, but nothing that impedes entry; Pláti baffles the prevailing wind and occasional swell.

LÉROS

Well-vegetated **Léros** ㊾, with its half-dozen deeply indented bays, looks like a jigsaw puzzle piece gone astray. **Lakkí** ㊿, the biggest, deepest inlet and large-ferry port, is graced by one of the world's largest Rationalist-Streamline Modern planned towns, designed as 'Porto Lago' by Rodolfo Petracco and Armando Bernabiti and erected during 1934–38 for the officers (and their families) of the huge nearby Italian naval base. The striking, photogenic, renovated buildings here include the round-fronted cinema, the market hall with its clock-tower and circular atrium, the arcaded primary school, and the angular church of Ágios Nikólaos.

Lakkí's present population of 2,058 (a quarter of Léros' inhabitants) rattles around the underused streets; nautical flavour is imparted by yacht marinas and dry-docks, here and at adjacent Teménia. The atmosphere was long weighted by three hospitals for disabled children and mentally unwell adults, though these institutions have mostly closed and the facilities partly occupied by the University of the Aegean's nursing faculty.

ITALIAN ARCHITECTURE IN THE DODECANESE

Italian rule left a significant architectural heritage, long neglected but recently appreciated and restored. These structures are often wrongly dubbed 'Art Deco'; while some display Art Deco traits, most are Rationalist or Streamline Modern. These schools emerged from early-1900s artistic and political trends, particularly Futurism, Fascist-inspired Novecento Italiano and the 1909–13 'Metaphysical Cities' series of painter Giorgio di Chirico (1888–1978).

During 1924–36, Italy attempted to combine Rationalism and real or imaginary vernacular elements into a generic Mediterranean architecture. Each Dodecanese got at least one specimen in this 'protectorate' synthesis, usually the police station or post office, but only four important islands (Rhodes, Kos, Kálymnos, Léros) experienced comprehensive urban re-ordering.

Kos and Kálymnos received a Foro Italico (administrative complex) in neo-Crusader style. Fascist theory also required a square for rallies (on Kos, Platía Eleftherías). 1936–41 was marked by intensified ideology and reference to the islands' Latin heritage (the Romans and their purported successors, the Knights Hospitaller). This entailed 'purification', removing orientalist ornamentation and replacing this with poros stone cladding. Additionally, severity and rigid symmetry – as in the Orthodox cathedral on Kos – was stipulated. Otherwise, Kos was curiously exempt from purification.

A controversial mural at Agía Kiourá

The rest of Léros is more conventionally inviting (easily toured by scooter), particularly the fishing/yacht port of **Pandéli**, with its fine-pebble beach and waterfront tavernas, just downhill from the capital of **Plátanos,** its pastel-hued vernacular houses draped over a saddle. Overhead looms a well-preserved **Knights' castle** (daily 8am–1pm and 4–8pm; charge) sheltering an excellent ecclesiastical museum (the English-speaking warden gives an engaging tour). The summit views, especially southeast at dusk, are superb.

South of Pandéli, **Vromólithos** ⑤ has the best easily accessible and car-free beach on an island lacking good, sandy ones. Elsewhere, sharp rock reefs must often be crossed entering the water. Southeast of Vromólithos, two sandy coves at **Ágios Geórgios** are less crowded.

Picturesque **Agia Marína** ⑤ , beyond Plátanos, is the usual excursion boat and catamaran harbour (though catamarans often dock at Lakkí). It has several tavernas and cafés, plus more whimsical Italian monuments like the market hall and customs house.

ÁLINDA AND AROUND

Álinda ⑤ , 3km (2 miles) northwest along the same bay via **Krithóni**, is Léros' oldest established resort, with a long pebble beach right by the road – quieter swimming is available east around the bay at **Panagiés** and **Dýo Liskária** (taverna-café). In a walled enclosure at Álinda's south end, a poignant, immaculately maintained **Commonwealth War Graves cemetery** contains 184 casualties of the Battle of Léros.

The other Álinda sight is the **Folklore and Historic Museum**, housed in the unmistakable Bellenis castle-mansion (May–mid-Sept Tue–Sun 9am–1pm and 6–8pm; charge). Many displays pertain to the battle: relics from the sunken Queen Olga, a Junkers bomber-wheel, a stove made from a bomb casing. There's also a rather grisly mock-up clinic and assorted rural impedimenta, costumes and antiques. One room is devoted to Communist artist Kyiakos Tsakiris (1915–98), interned locally by the junta, his works executed on stones, shells and wood. Photos recall vanished monuments: a fine market hall in Plátanos demolished in 1903, and a soaring medieval aqueduct at the Kástro destroyed during the 1943 battle.

REMOTE SITES

In antiquity Léros was sacred to Artemis, though her temple is lost somewhere near the airport – definitely not the signposted foundations of an ancient fort. Artemis' reputed virginity survives in the place-name **Parthéni**, past the airport: an infamous political prison during the 1967–74 junta, now a grim army base, as it was in Italian times. Things perk up beyond, at **Blefoútis** beach (taverna), plus the hilltop chapel of **Agía Kiourá** 🔞 (always open), decorated by Tsakiris and two other junta-era prisoners with strikingly heterodox murals of Christ's Passion and the Apostles, which the mainstream Church has always loathed – they are legally protected from further erasure.

Other bays tend not to be worth the effort. West-facing **Goúrna** has a long, sandy and gently shelving (but also windy and often dirty) beach. Isolated, southerly **Xirókambos** refuses to face the

The Monastery of St John the Theologian on Pátmos

fact that its scrappy beach hinders its chances of becoming a proper resort; caiques ply to and from Myrtiés (Kálymnos) daily in season, but it's better to continue to Pandéli (four times weekly). For more variety in swimming spots, take a **day cruise** (11am–7pm; €25–30) with the Barbarossa, moored at Agía Marína, to various islets northwest of Léros.

LÉROS WAR MUSEUMS

The Merikiá Tunnel Museum (daily 9.30am–1.30pm; charge), occupying the former Italian naval command centre, displays abundant, barely labelled documents and military hardware; histrionically narrated archival footage tries to explain everything. Either Ioannis Paraponiaris' Deposito di Guerra in remote Agía Iríni, or Tassos Kanaris' private collection in Plátanos, makes better viewing; guided tours only, easiest arranged through Léros Active in Agía Marína (tel: 22470 24590). The massive Italian radio-command buildings at Ágios Nikólaos are unlocked, with Nazi insignia painted on the walls inside.

PÁTMOS

Pátmos ⑤ has been synonymous with the biblical Book of Revelation (Apocalypse) ever since tradition placed its authorship here, in AD 95, by John the Evangelist. A volcanic landscape, with evocative rock formations and sweeping views, seems suitably apocalyptic. In 1088 the monk Hristodoulos Latrenos founded a Patmian monastery in honour of St John the Theologian (as John the Evangelist is known in Greek;

Theologos is a common island male name), which soon became a focus of scholarship and pilgrimage. A Byzantine imperial charter granted the monastery tax exemption and the right to engage in trade, concessions respected by later overlords.

Although the monks no longer rule Pátmos, their presence tempers potential resort rowdiness. While there are some naturist beaches, nightlife is genteel, and the clientele upmarket (including the Aga Khan's family, plus various ruling or deposed royal families). Those who elect to stay overnight appreciate the

THE BATTLE OF LÉROS

Across Léros bomb nose-cones and shell casings serve as gaily painted courtyard ornaments or gateposts – evidence of the 1943 **Battle of Léros**. The British landed forces on 13 September, who (together with the existing Italian garrison) attempted to hold Léros. Over 52 days from 26 September – when the destroyers Intrepid (British) and Queen Olga (Greek) were sunk at Lakkí – the Germans bombarded the island with 1,369 air-sorties from Rhodes and Greece's mainland. Besides 'softening up' British Commonwealth HQ at Merovígli above Plátanos, a principal objective was to knock out monstrous, hilltop Italian guns, whose range of ten nautical miles made approach by sea impossible.

Finally, on 12 November, the Germans began landing both paratroops and fighters shipped to the northeast coast, where Allied gunnery sank two landing craft. An unusually warm autumn created even more hellish conditions. German mastery of the air made resupply of the island impossible, and ensured the Allied loss of Léros. On 16 November, the British commander surrendered, with 8,500 Commonwealth and Italian soldiers taken prisoner. Casualties on all sides were horrendous – 80 from the Queen Olga's crew; about 400 Italians, from their force of about 8,000; about 600 Commonwealth, out of roughly 3,000; and 2,600 Germans (most lost at sea).

Monastery of St John the Theologian fresco

unique, even spiritual, atmosphere that Pátmos exudes once day-trippers and cruise-ship patrons have departed.

Skála 56 is the port and largest village, best appreciated at night when crickets serenade and yacht-masts glow against a dark sky. By day Skála loses its charm, but all island commerce is based here. The modern town dates only from the 1820s, when the Aegean had largely been cleared of pirates, but at the summit of the westerly rise, known as Kastélli (signposted), lie extensive foundations of an ancient acropolis.

Buses leave regularly from the quay for the hilltop **Hóra**, but a 40-minute cobbled path short-cutting the road (or a longer trail shown on the recommended map) is preferable in cool weather, at least downhill. Hóra's core, protected by massive, pirate-proof fortifications and visible from a great distance, is **Agíou Ioánnou tou Theológou Monastery** (Monastery of St John the Theologian; daily 8am–1.30pm, Tue, Thu, Sat also 4–6pm), hopelessly packed out when cruise-ship groups arrive – time visits accordingly. A photogenic maze of interlinked courtyards, stairways, chapels and passageways, it occupies the site of an ancient temple, duly admired by Hristodoulos and his work party before they demolished it to recycle its masonry. The Treasury (charge) houses the most impressive monastic collection in Greece outside Mount Athos. Among precious icons and jewellery, the prize exhibit is the edict of Emperor Alexios Komnenos granting the island to Hristodoulos. The narthex of the main church, to your left as you enter the monastery, has excellent late-medieval **frescoes** by Cretan painters, mostly scenes from the life and miracles of Hristodoulos.

Hóra ❺❼ village grew up outside the monastery from the 1280s onwards. Despite earthquakes and Italian demolitions, it remains architecturally homogenous, with cobbled, occasionally arcaded alleys lined by shipowners' mansions dating from Pátmos' 17th- and 18th-century heyday, bought by wealthy outsiders decades ago. High, almost windowless walls and monumental wooden doors betray nothing of the opulence within: painted ceilings, pebble-mosaic terraces, flagstoned kitchens with carved cistern heads, antique furniture, embroidered bed-curtains.

Away from the main thoroughfares and approaches to St John you stumble upon rarely disturbed passages, no wider than one person, lined with ruins or overgrown with fragrant marvel-of-Peru. On summer nights, when the monastery walls are floodlit, Hóra ranks as the most beautiful settlement in the Dodecanese.

From **Platía Lótza** in the north there is one of the most sweeping views in the Aegean, taking in multiple land-masses: going clockwise, Ikaría, Thýmena, Foúrni, Sámos, Arkí, Lipsí and double-humped Samsun Dağ (ancient Mount Mykale) in Turkey.

Just over halfway down the path from Hóra to Skála, smaller **Apokálypsis Monastery** (same hours as main monastery) was built around the grotto where John had his Revelation. A silver band on the wall marks the spot where John lay his head, while the divine Voice spoke through a great cleft in the rock above.

BEACHES

Pátmos's remote beaches are surprisingly good, with islet-spangled seascapes offshore and (usually) excellent tavernas. Buses ply between **Grikou** resort (**Pétra** beach immediately south is better) and northerly **Kámbos** bay, popular with Greek families. The biggest pure-sand cove is exposed but gently shelving **Psili Ammos ⑤⑧** in the far south, accessible by a half-hour marked trail. Beaches north of Skála, most on the sheltered 'inner' coastline, include (in order) sandy **Meloï**, with the island campsite; long **Agriolivádi**; sandy **Vagiá** beyond Kámbos, having the cleanest water; pebbly, double-cove **Lingínou**, popular with nudists; isolated **Livádi Geranoú ⑤⑨**, sand and gravel, with an islet to swim to; and finally **Lámbi ⑥⓪**, with irresistible, multi-coloured volcanic pebbles (it's forbidden to collect them).

Excursion boats from the northwest end of Skála quay offer **day-trips** (typically depart 9am, return at 5pm), to the islets of **Maráthi ⑥①**, **Arkí ⑥②** and **Lipsí ⑥③** northeast of Pátmos. With a long sandy beach and two tavernas, Maráthi is a relaxing choice.

BODRUM (TURKEY)

Kos and its neighbours are close to Turkey's southwestern coast, so day-trips there are widely offered. You'll need your passport for entry/exit formalities, but unless you stay overnight, UK nationals do not require a visa. Although Turkey uses the Turkish lira, almost all transactions – particularly souvenir purchases – can be conducted (at a slight mark-up) in euro or sterling.

The nearest Turkish port to Kos is **Bodrum**, 40 minutes away. Several companies offer day-trips from Mandráki quay, so competition is fierce. Departures are typically at 9 and 10am, with returns from Bodrum at 4 and 5pm, allowing six hours in Turkey.

Upon clearing immigration, head straight to the nearby, massive **Castle of St Peter**, built by the Knights Hospitaller 1402–1522. This now houses the **Museum of Underwater Archaeology**

(late Mar–Oct Tue–Sun 8am–6.30pm, bodrum-museum.com; charge), one of the best of its type, arrayed over several galleries. Unmissable are the Uluburun Wreck Hall, featuring treasures recovered from the oldest (14th-century BC) known shipwreck, and the Carian Princess Hall, exhibiting the remains and effects of a local 4th-century BC noblewoman, including a gold diadem, drinking cup and jewellery.

Bodrum's other main attraction is its **bazaar** – a warren of lanes inland and northeast from the castle, either side of Cevat Şakir Caddesi. Mass-

Castle of St Peter, Bodrum

produced trinkets predominate, along with spices, leather goods, jewellery, beads, and shoddily made counterfeit designer apparel. A sense of humour is useful, as sales tactics are intense, and prices not necessarily cheaper than on Kos.

Allow time for strolling through Bodrum's residential districts, inland from the yacht anchorage, with their whitewashed, cubist houses, overgrown by bougainvillea and other subtropical vegetation. Come lunch-time, better value can be found away from the waterfront – for example at Otantik Ocakbaşı on Atatürk Cad 12/B, Kumbahçe, inland from the east beach, or Nazık Ana, at Eski Hükümet Sok 7 in the bazaar. Many menu items are the same as on Kos – only the name changes, and even then not always. Greeks and Turks have lived together for almost a millennium, and their cultures are more similar than some would admit.

WHAT TO DO

Kos and its neighbours are not just excellent holiday destinations in terms of scenery, historical sites and museums – they offer assorted sporting, shopping and entertainment opportunities.

SPORTS

There are plenty of occasions for an active holiday on Kos or surrounding smaller islands, both on land and at sea. Beaches – whether sandy, pebbly or a mixture – and swimming are covered in the Where to Go section. Sea-surface temperatures attain 26°C/79°F in August/September; water cleanliness is usually among the best in the Aegean.

WATERSPORTS

Kos, as you'll soon notice, is a very breezy place, with reliable prevailing northwesterly winds. Accordingly, windsurfing and kitesurfing is avidly practiced. The best spots are around Cape Psalídi in the far northeast, Marmári and Kohylári on the northwest-facing coast, and southeast-facing Kéfalos Bay.

Established centres for instruction and equipment rental include Windzone, Psalídi (www.windzone-kos.gr, tel: 6939 117475 or 6979 723193); Big Blue Surf Center, Psalídi (www. bigblue-surfcenter.gr, tel: 6945 898232); Marmari Windsurfing, behind the Marmari Beach Hotel (www.marmari-windsurfing. com, tel: 6940 607280); Kohilari Kite Center, at Kohylári beach near Limniónas (email kefaloskite@yahoo.gr, 6944 736939) and Kefalos Windsurfing, Kéfalos Bay (www.kefaloswind surfing.com, tel: 6977 620316).

Scuba courses and dive trips are offered from Kos, but with principally sandy shallows there is little to see nearby;

Hiking towards Sikati beach, on Kálymnos

even one of the dive centres admits that their emphasis is on certification, not expeditions. Conditions are better around Kálymnos, but the best diving in the region is to be had off Léros, which is surrounded by extensive military debris – German, Italian, Greek and British – from the autumn 1943 Battle of Léros, much of it between 30 and 60 metres deep. Thus only intermediate and advanced divers can visit the wrecks of the Greek destroyer *Queen Olga*; a British landing craft; a Junkers 52 transport airplane; an anti-submarine-net tender; and the submarine net itself. Shallower wrecks accessible to novice divers include a German landing craft; a Heinkel 111 bomber; and an Arado 198 seaplane.

Two reputable Kos dive centres are Kos Divers in Psalídi (www.kosdivers.com, tel: 6932 155422), with PADI Open Water certification courses for €490, and Arian Diving Centre in Kardámena (www.arian-diving-centre.com, tel: 22420 92465), with certifications at €450. Kálymnos has two centres, Divers Island (tel: 6948 376039, www.diversisland-kalymnos.gr) and Kalymnos Diving (tel: 22430 47890, www.kalymnosdiving.gr). On Léros, there is just one dive operator, Hydrovius in Krithóni (tel: 22470 25679), which prefers that you book through Léros Active Travel (www.lerosactive.com, tel: 22470 24590). They offer 10-dive packages to qualified divers at an attractive price of €300.

HIKING

Kos does not have much of a path network – it's too cultivated and developed; the unmissable ascent of Hristós peak is detailed on page 58. Kálymnos by contrast has a good, well-documented network of paths, providing excellent walking during the cooler months. The same is true of Nísyros, and to a lesser extent Pátmos, where routes have recently been marked. With the exception of Kálymnos (Anavasi map

Kos's waters teem with war and ordinary wrecks

10.32, scale 1:25,000; www.mountains.gr), these islands are adequately covered by Terrain maps (www.terrainmaps.gr) at scales of 1:20,000–1:25,000 (1:45,000 for Kos).

MOUNTAIN-BIKING

Kos may not be a hiking destination, but with numerous dirt-surface forest and ravine tracks of a moderate grade, it is fine for mountain-biking during the cooler months, as are adjacent Nísyros and Kálymnos. Kos Bike Activities in Psalídi (tel: 6944 150129, www.kosbikeactivities.com) offers guided tours four days weekly on Kos, once a week on Nísyros and once weekly on Kálymnos. Most itineraries, on Scott-brand bikes with other essentials supplied, are rated difficult and at least partially off-road; cost €46–58 per person.

ROCK-CLIMBING

The cliffs of Kálymnos and its satellite islet Télendos afford some of the most exciting big-wall climbing in Europe.

Since the late 1990s, the international climbing fraternity has effectively extended the tourist season on these islands back to March and forward into November, avoiding being baked to a crisp on the palisades during high summer. There are literally scores of routes, mostly from Masoúri north to Skália; two good sources of information are www.kalymnoslimbing.eu, affiliated with a particular climbing school, and the more disinterested www.climbkalymnos.com, with a guidebook on sale.

THE GENUINE ICON

Icons (Greek *ikónes*) are images of saints, prophets, archangels or apostles, or episodes in Christ's or the Virgin's life. They are not intended as naturalistic depictions of holy personalities, whose unvarying attributes – hairstyle, instruments of martyrdom, clothing – were fixed early in Christianity.

Icons form the heart of Orthodox worship, as a focus for prayer and a 'window' to the saint being petitioned. All are considered sacred; some reputedly possess miraculous powers. The oldest surviving examples date from after 843 AD.

Icon-painters created works for private clients as well as for churches, and they were popular souvenirs for Grand Tourists and religious pilgrims. However, modern production methods, including the use of thin canvas and synthetic colours, saw them lose favour. But lately traditional painting methods have been revived, both for church renovations and for commercial sale. Powdered natural pigments, vinegar and egg yolk are painstakingly mixed to form tempera, then brushed onto sturdy stretched canvas or even a solid plank. Gold leaf is then applied, and the whole image given a patina. Such time-consuming work is exquisite and correspondingly expensive.

HORSE-RIDING

There are several horse-riding stables on Kos, offering either foothill jaunts or beach itineraries. The oldest (since 1992) and largest stables, with Hungarian, French and Andalusian horses, is family-run Salt Lake Stables near Marmári, just southwest of said salt lake (http://horse ridingkos.wix.com/horse ridingkos, tel: 6944 104446, May–early Nov), with small groups, young kids or nov-

Horse-riding at sunset

ices catered for, free transfers and full equipment provided. Sunrise/sunset and moonlight rides along the nearby beach are their speciality; budget €40 for a two-hour dawn/dusk ride, €50 for two hours by moonlight.

SHOPPING

The Greek islands are not a shopper's paradise like Morocco, India, Mexico or other exotic realms, but there are still many things that make nice souvenirs or gifts.

Antiques. Very few genuine antiquities (officially classified as anything made before 1821) are sold. These are usually ceramics, jewellery or icons, and will require authentication certificates and an export permit – the dealer should be able to advise you in this process. For those whose budget does not stretch to such items, there are many reproductions, of varying quality and price. Skála on Pátmos, with cruise-ship patrons coming ashore, has a few shops stocking knick-knacks from a century ago, but don't expect any bargains.

Souvenir shopping in Kos Town

Carpets and rag-rugs. Any oriental carpets sold on Kos are imported from Turkey, via Bodrum opposite. You may as well go on a day-trip and secure a rug in person, being mindful of regulations concerning duty-free import value (VAT may still be payable in Greece) – currently €430 worth of goods per adult. Obtain realistic invoices for the goods in Bodrum – Greek customs officials know the market.

Indigenous weaving traditions on Kos and its neighbours have all but died out. You might see – more likely in a homewares shop than a tourist boutique – brightly coloured *koureloúdes* (rag-rugs), which can be good value. Older ones have more subdued hues and tighter weave, and are thus priced accordingly. Tasteful *koureloúdes* have been sold in the past at *Barba Stathis* taverna on Télendos islet, off Kálymnos.

Most of the cotton rugs and bathmats on display, with Aegean motifs such as dolphins framed by a geometric meander pattern, are mass-produced and imported (usually from India). That said, such mats are cheap, hard-wearing and do not shrink much.

Ceramics and sculpture. Kos still has a small pottery industry, with shops in the main town, Lagoúdi and Ziá. Plates, jugs, cups and bowls are produced in a variety of patterns and colours. Skála on Pátmos is also promising for ceramics shopping. Miniature copies of Classical sculptures are also popular. Prices vary according to quality of the materials and the workmanship. You will soon discern this after visiting a few different stores and closely examining items.

Clothing. Kos has plenty of outlets for summery cotton or muslin trousers, tops and dresses. You will also find plenty of T-shirts, swimwear and beach footwear. The traditional August sales now start in July, but you'll be lucky to find something in the most common sizes.

Jewellery. You can choose as many carats in precious stones as your budget can handle. Gold and silver are sold by weight, with relatively little extra cost added for the workmanship. In the lower price ranges there is plenty of everyday jewellery such as ankle chains in metal or leather, navel studs and rings.

Leather items. There are plenty of handbags, wallets and belts on sale in all resorts, of widely differing material and workmanship. A quality woman's handbag costs upwards of €40.

Olive wood items. Olive wood can be laboriously carved or lathe-turned into practical souvenirs, ranging from coasters or flat-candle holders to large salad bowls, smaller cereal bowls or cutting boards, the latter fairly expensive (€20–35 for a board, €18–50 for a bowl). Pricier items are more likely (though not

A vast choice of olive wood kitchenware

Soumáda for sale on Nísyros

guaranteed) to be from fully cured wood, which resists cracking; green olive wood is more popular with craftsman because it's easier to work, but invariably develops fatal splits after a couple of years as it finishes drying in your home. Cutting boards should be one-piece, not glued sections. Protect your investment by oiling it occasionally with olive oil, and never leaving it immersed in water.

Food and drink. Fruit – especially sour cherries, figs, plums and Seville oranges – are preserved in jars as *glyká koutalioú* or 'spoon sweets'. Nísyros is the place to score a jar of pickled caper greens, a great accent to any salad, or on their own.

Bees frequent aromatic hillside herbs on Kos, Kálymnos and Léros, producing delicious honey. Kalymnian honey is arguably the best available on the islands in this guide. But beware – there is no quality control of the industry, and adulteration is rife. Always taste first before buying, if possible. Much of what is touted as 'thyme honey' isn't. Genuine thyme honey is highly aromatic, and when a jar or can is opened the distinctive aroma should waft out.

Olives are preserved either in oil or brine, or made into unadulterated 'extra virgin' (first, cold pressing) oil for cooking and delicious salad dressings. Hatzipetros or Papadimitriou are the major bottlers on Kos, with their products ubiquitous.

A distinctively Greek drink to take home is anise-or-fennel-flavoured oúzo – the best comes from the islands of Sámos (Giokarinis or Frantzeskos brands) and Lésvos (too many distillers to list). Go for *apóstagma* (purely distilled). Many of the better Greek wines can be found at Marinos bottle shops, with outlets on Kálymnos (Póthia waterfront, tel: 22470 22093) and in Kos Town (tel: 22420 41940).

On Nísyros, two non-alcoholic drink bases are made and sold. *Soumáda* is almond syrup, sadly no longer made from island almonds but imported ones. Diluted 4:1 with chilled water, it's supremely refreshing. Somewhat less so and more cloying is local *kaneláda*, a red, cinnamon-laced syrup, which tastes a little like dentist's mouthwash.

WINE VARIETIES AND TASTING

Kos has several commercial wineries, some equipped for visits. Hatziemmanouil, on the trunk road just southwest of the main Tingáki turning (tel: 22420 68888, www.hatziemmanouil.gr; May–Oct daily 9am–7pm, otherwise by arrangement), is the most established, with six labels available. Tops is their Red Syrah (13.5 percent), aged one year in oak barrels; the Cabernet/Syrah blend (13 percent) is cheaper. They also make two whites and a dessert wine.

The Triantafyllopoulos winery nearby (tel: 22420 69860, www.kos winery.gr; May–Oct Mon–Sat 8.30am–5pm) has plusher tasting facilities, with fine views over vineyards to the sea. They offer eight labels, the most interesting being whites of *athíri-asýrtiko* or sauvignon blanc-*malagouziá* blends, an oak-aged red (13.5 percent) of blended tempranillo, syrah and cabernet franc, and an outstanding rosé of grenache rouge and syrah.

Hatzinikolaou (tel: 6945 372999) does not yet have tasting facilities but their popular products (eight reds) are widely available in local supermarkets; go for their Sapphire Blue Syrah (12 percent) and Platanaki (12 percent), a blend of Merlot and Mavrothílyko, an heirloom grape rescued from extinction on Nísyros.

WINERY TOURISM

Commercial wine-making on Kos collapsed in 1998 with the bankruptcy of the Vinko co-operative. Since 2004, however, the slack has been taken up admirably by a handful of private wineries, some producing 50,000–80,000 bottles per year. Unusually for a Greek island, Kos excels particularly at dry red wines, made from legacy Greek grapes, imported varieties or blends. There are also newish wineries on Léros and Pátmos.

ENTERTAINMENT

MUSIC AND DANCE

The rich and varied Greek musical tradition goes back hundreds of years, originally based on Byzantine chant but in modern times featuring wonderful settings of popular poetry to music. Each region of Greece has its particular songs and dances;

Kos Town nightlife

those of the southeastern islands, including Kos and its neighbours, are called *nisió-tika*. Some tavernas or bars host live traditional music, typically on Wednesday, Friday and Saturday evenings. Genuine folk dancing is now difficult to witness, but more likely at a private wedding or saint's day when perfor-mances occur in their true context (see Calendar of Events on page 97).

Summer cinema

Cine Orfeas, Fenaréti 3, Kos Town (www.cine-orfeas.gr, tel: 22420 25713; early June to late Sept/early Oct) is one of the loveliest outdoor cinemas in Greece. Screenings are nightly at 9pm and/or 11.15pm. Sit back with a box of popcorn and enjoy last year's releases. Admission €7; some hotels provide discount vouchers.

NIGHTLIFE (AND DAYLIFE)

The best concentrations for lively bars on Kos are along Aktí Andoníou Zouroúdi, the main drag of the Lámbi seafront; the so-called 'Bar Lanes' just in from Mandráki port; and the back-streets of Kardámena. On Nísyros, the Lefkandió water-front in Mandráki is typically hopping after dark, while classic, durable bars on Léros include Savana at Pandéli and Café del Mar at Vromólithos. The profile on Kálymnos and Pátmos is much more fluid at present. In terms of big, hi-tech clubs, X at Kanári 2 in Kos Town, and Starlight at the edge of Kardámena, are likely to survive the current economic climate.

A well-loved Greek institution are all-day beach bars with DJ'd music. They generally get going around noon and keep on until the small hours. On Kos, three good ones are Mylos on Aktí Andoníou Zouroúdi, Ammos in Psalídi (Fri live events) and Aplo at the edge of Mastihári (Wed live music).

Kos has a summer (late June–Aug) festival, the Hippo-krateia, but this has no website, Facebook page or printed

Children love a castle

advance programme. Stop by the tourist information office, or look out for posters. Events comprise re-enactments of folk customs, exhibits and concerts.

CHILDREN'S KOS

Kos and surrounding islands are great places to take kids. Greek society is very family-orientated, and children will be indulged in cafés and tavernas. Most Kos resort hotels have a range of child-friendly activities, including kids' clubs, designated swimming areas and playgrounds.

Since the Mediterranean has very little tide, and Kos and Pátmos in particular have many gently shelving bays, there are lots of safe places for children to paddle. Sandy beaches are more fun than pebbly ones for castle-building and hole-digging; our beach coverage distinguishes the two.

For older children, the Knights' castles on Kos, Nísyros, Kálymnos and Léros will prove fascinating; the volcanic crater on Nísyros should also be a hit, as will the peacocks of Pláka Forest. The recommended Kos riding stable accepts all ages, with ponies for youngsters. Watersports offered at most resorts across the island – standup paddle-boarding, kayaking, windsurfing – provide a more active challenge. For a fun family day out, try Lido Water Park near Mastihári (daily May–Oct 10am–6.30pm; tel: 22420 59241, www.lidowaterpark.com), with a multi-lane slide, lazy river, special kids area and several pools including a wave pool.

CALENDAR OF EVENTS

1 January: *Protohroniá*/St Basil's Day; the traditional greeting is Kalí Hroniá.

6 January: *Ta Theofánia*/Epiphany, the Baptism of Christ; young men dive into the sea to recover a crucifix; the retriever is considered lucky.

7 March: 1948 Union of Dodecanese with Greece: parades, dancing.

Clean Monday: 48 days before Easter, start of Lenten fast (no meat or cheese); kite-flying and countryside outings.

25 March: Greek Independence Day/Festival of the Annunciation.

Easter: the most important Orthodox holiday. Maundy Thursday eve features the moving Crucifixion Mass; on Good Friday, processions in each parish follow the flower-decked bier of Christ. The midnight Resurrection Mass on Holy Saturday concludes with fireworks and the relaying of the sacred flame from officiating priests to parishioners. On Sunday roast lambs end the Lenten fast.

1 May: *Protomagiá*/May Day: flower-gathering excursions to the country – and massive parades by the political Left.

May/June variable: *Agíou Pnévmatos*/Holy Spirit (Whit) Monday. National holiday concludes a three-day weekend.

14–15 August: *Kímisi tis* Theotókou/Dormition of the Virgin. Processions and festivals wherever there is a church dedicated to this feast (some Marian churches celebrate 8 September or 21 November).

29 August: *Apotomí Timías Kefalís Prodrómou*/Beheading of John the Baptist; pilgrimage and celebration at his monastery near Kéfalos, Kos.

14 September *Ýpsosi tou Timíou Stavroú*/Elevation of the Holy Cross, observed on Nísyros.

25–26 September *Metástasi Ioánni Theológou*/Departure of St John the Theologian, at his monasteries on Pátmos and Nísyros.

28 October: *Óhi* (No) Day, commemorating Greek defiance of the Italian invasion in 1940.

25–26 December *Hristoúgenna*/Christmas. The traditional symbol, in public squares, is an illuminated boat.

New Year's Eve: A cake (the *vassilópita*) is baked with a coin hidden inside – bringing good luck to whoever gets that slice.

EATING OUT

Greek cuisine relies on seasonal ingredients at peak flavour and freshness, served raw, or cooked simply – on a grill, flash-fried or slow baked. Greeks have long cherished staples like olive oil, cheese, yoghurt, wild greens, seafood and free-range meat, along with garden vegetables, fruit, pulses and nuts. The traditional Greek diet is among the healthiest in the world.

WHERE TO EAT

On Kos and its neighbours you find several types of eateries, each emphasising certain dishes; don't expect oven-cooked casseroles at a seaside grill, or at an *ouzerí*. Many resort restaurants offer bland fare aimed at timid palates; for more authentic, good-value cuisine, refer to the recommendations section (see page 107).

The *psistariá* offers charcoal-grilled meats, plus a limited selection of salads and *mezédes*. The *tavérna* has a more elaborate menu, offering pre-cooked, steam-tray dishes known as *magireftá*, as well as some grills and salads.

An *ouzerí* purveys not just the famous anise (*glykániso*) or fennel-flavoured tipple, but also the *mezédes* dishes that complement it – thus the common alias *mezedopolío*. *Oúzo* is never drunk by itself; octopus, olives, a bit of cheese or nuts are traditional accompaniments, but there are numerous other possibilities.

The *kafenío* (coffee shop) is traditionally an exclusively male domain, and still is in the deep countryside. Often very plainly decorated

Dreaded bread

Taverna bread is often inedible, and you have the right to refuse, and not pay for, it; some wait staff ask foreigners if they actually want bread. Bread/starch consumption is, however, deeply engrained locally, and Greeks habitually scoff bread *and* potatoes *and* rice or pasta at the same meal.

(though tables and chairs have gotten smarter), they host political discussions and backgammon games. Only drinks are served.

WHEN TO EAT

Resort tavernas open for lunch and dinner; some offer a full breakfast. Typically, Greeks don't eat breakfast – a coffee and a baked pastry is as much as they indulge in. English/American-style breakfasts are only available in major resorts and fancier hotels. Lunch is taken between 2.30 and 4pm, before shops open again at around

There's no shortage of tavernas

5.30pm. Dinner is usually eaten from 9.30pm onwards; some establishments will take last orders after midnight.

Tourist-orientated tavernas begin evening service at around 6.30pm. You will have your choice of table if you sit down before 7.30pm, but the atmosphere is definitely better later on when locals come out to eat.

WHAT TO EAT

Extensive, multilingual menus indicate available items with a price pencilled in adjacent. The menu is most useful for checking that the taverna is in your price range for items like meat or fish; a more reliable account of that day's offerings can be obtained from your waiter. Check also the steam-trays or chiller case to see what looks enticing.

All restaurants levy a 'cover charge'. This is essentially for a serving of bread and is rarely over €1 per person.

APPETISERS

Carefully selected appetisers *(mezédes)* can constitute a full meal. Shared by the whole table, they are a fun way to eat – simply order as many platters as you want. *Ouzerís/mezedopolía* have no qualms about purveying *mezédes*-only meals, bringing ready-made choices out on a *dískos* or tray – though they also serve hot main courses to order *(tis óras)*.

The most common appetisers are *tzatzíki*, yoghurt dip flavoured with garlic, cucumber and mint; *florínes* or *piperiés kérates gemistés*, red or green peppers stuffed with cheese; *yaprákia*, vine leaves stuffed with rice, herbs and sometimes mince – which can be served hot (with *avgolémono* or egg-lemon sauce) or cold (with yoghurt); *lahanodolmádes*, cabbage leaves

Catch of the day

stuffed with rice and mince, often under *avgolémono* sauce; *taramosaláta*, cod-roe paste blended with breadcrumbs or mashed potato, olive oil and lemon juice, ideally beige and not dyed pink; *melitzanosaláta* (aubergine purée, ideally without mayonnaise – ask); *anthí* (stuffed squash blossoms, often battered); *kolokythokeftédes* (courgette rissoles); *kalamarákia gónos*, fried hatchling squid; *tyrokafterí* or *kopanistí*, two kinds of spicy cheese dips; *plevrótous* (grilled oyster mushrooms); *bekrí mezé* (pork chunks in spicy sauce); and *hórta*, boiled greens (wild chicories or endive in spring/autumn, farm-raised *vlíta* or Amaranthus viridis during summer). *Saganáki* is yellow cheese coated in breadcrumbs and then fried, while *féta psití* is feta cheese baked in foil with garlic, tomato and hot peppers.

Proper Greek chips

No taverna with any professional pride or hopes of courting local diners shrinks from the task of making hand-cut, fresh chips daily, as opposed to frozen pre-packed imports. Piping hot, regularly changed oil and thorough draining are obvious in the result.

Greek salad or *horiátiki saláta* (usually translated as 'village salad') consists of tomato, cucumber, onion, green peppers and olives topped with feta cheese. On Nísyros especially sprigs of brine-preserved caper leaves (*kápari*) often adorn Greek salads, which are portioned for two.

Cruets of olive oil (*ládi*) and wine vinegar (*xýdi*) are found with salt, pepper and napkins on the table.

FISH

You choose from the fish displayed on ice. This is then weighed before cooking – check the price as seafood is usually expensive. Frozen seafood (likely from July to September) must be so indicated on the menu – though often cryptically with a 'k' or an asterisk. The idiom for wild, free-range fish is *alaniáriko*.

Moussaká

Larger fish are usually grilled and smaller fish fried, then served with fresh lemon and *ladolémono* (olive oil with lemon juice). Common species are *barboúni* (red mullet), *koutsoumoúra* (another mullet), *skorpína* (scorpion-fish, baked, in soup or grilled), *koliós* (chub mackerel), *bakaliáros* (fresh hake, also rehydrated), *xifías* (swordfish), *tsipoúra* (gilt-head bream) and *fangrí* (bream) – the latter two often farmed. A Kos treat is *filipáki* (no translation), a blunt-headed, sand-bank-dwelling little fellow served fried, not very meaty but delicately flavoured. *Marídes/maridáki* (picarel), *gávros* (anchovy) and *atherína* (sand smelt) are also served crisp-fried by the portion, while *sardélles* (sardines) are often grilled. More elaborate seafood dishes include *soupiá* (cuttlefish), *khtapódi xydáto* (marinated octopus salad), or *garídes saganáki* (prawns in cheese sauce).

MEAT AND CASSEROLE DISHES

Meaty snacks include *gýros* (pork slivers cut from a vertical cone), and *souvláki* (small chunks of meat), either served with tomato, *tzatzíki* and chips in pitta bread. Whole chickens or bigger chunks of lamb and pork are rotisseried on a *souvlá* (skewer) as sit-down mains. Pork or veal *brizóla* is a cutlet; lamb or goat chops, however, are *païdákia. Pansétta* are spare ribs, the cheapest meat mains around besides *loukánika* (sausages).

In these economically fraught times, *sykotákia arnísia* (lamb liver chunks) are inexpensive and popular, as are chicken livers (*sykotákia poulerikón*).

Greece's most famous oven dish is *moussakás* – sliced potato, aubergine and minced lamb topped with béchamel sauce. It should be firm but succulent, and redolent of nutmeg. *Pastítsio* is another layered recipe with macaroni, mince and cheese sauce. Other common casseroles include *giouvétsi* (meat baked in a clay pot with *kritharáki* pasta – Italian *orzo*) and *papoutsáki* (eggplant 'shoes' stuffed with mince).

Hot vegetarian dishes include *gemistá*, tomatoes, or peppers filled with herb-flavoured rice; *melitzánes imám*, aubergine stuffed with tomato, onion, and garlic; or *briám/tourloú* (ratatouille). Vegetarian *yaprákia*, more common than meaty ones, are called *gialantzí* ('liar's').

CHEESES

Greek cheeses (*tyriá*) are made from cow's, ewe's or goat's milk, or often blends. *Féta* cheese is ubiquitous, atop every salad or served with olive oil and oregano. *Graviéra* is a common hard cheese, varying in sharpness; milder (semi-)soft cheeses such as *manoúri*, *myzithra* or *anthótyro* are served plain or used for stuffing.

DESSERT

Most tavernas bring you a *kérazma* or sweet on the house together with the bill. This might be a plate of fresh seasonal fruit, semolina halva (*simigdalísios halvás*) or chocolate loaf (*kormós*). Postprandial

Kos specialities

Kos has some 'indigenous' dishes which you won't find on other islands. *Pinigoúri* is bulgur wheat, by itself or as the basis of meat casseroles. *Pikhtí* is pork brawn, usually served cold, while *krasotýri* or *póssa* is hard goat cheese aged in red wine – pungent going on its own, better as a stuffing.

Coffee and sweets

fruit platters feature water-melon or Persian melon in summer, grapes or pears in autumn, sliced apple in winter and citrus, kiwi slices or maybe strawberries in spring.

Elsewhere, *zaharoplastía* (sticky-cake shops) dish out decadent sweets, legacies of the Ottomans: *baklavás*, layers of honey-soaked flaky pastry with walnuts; *kataïfi*, shredded wheat filled with chopped almonds and honey; *galaktoboúreko*, custard pie; or *ravaní*, honey-soaked sponge cake.

For dairy desserts, try *ryzógalo*, cold rice pudding, or *kréma* (custard) at a *galaktopolío* (dairy shop). A quality ice-cream (*pagotó*) cult is well established in the Dodecanese; the best outlets on Kos are Paradosi, in Platáni village, and Special, Vassiléos Georgíou 7, Kos Town (plus 3 branches). On Léros try Elliniko in Agía Marína; on Pátmos, DeSantis/Marechiaro is tops.

WHAT TO DRINK

Greek winemaking dates back four millennia; quality, especially at certain mainland vintners, has risen dramatically in recent decades, but owing to limited export – many boutique wineries produce fewer than 30,000 bottles annually – the best labels are unknown abroad. Kos wine is more than respectable, and featured at most tavernas.

The cheapest wine is *hýma* or *varelísio* (in bulk), usually from the mainland. Red, white or rosé are given in full, half- or quarter-litre measures. Quality varies considerably; ask to taste-test first. Diluting with canned soda makes the harshest wine quaffable, but also gets you drunk quicker.

Retsína has been around since ancient times, when Greeks discovered the preservative properties of pine resin for storing wine. It can be an acquired taste and should be served well chilled. Purists state, though, that no true *retsína* exists beyond the mainland; the best bottled brand is Georgiadi from Thessaloníki. Avoid CAIR (Rhodes) *retsína*.

Oúzo is taken as an aperitif with ice and water; the anethole in it turns the mixture cloudy. On Kos and its neighbours, the most popular brands come from the islands of Lésvos or Sámos. Similar distillates are tsikoudiá (from Crete, anise-free) and mainland tsípouro (with or without glykániso). Thanks to cross-border tourism, Turkish rakí is popular on Kos and Léros.

There are nine mass-market beers produced in Greece, as well as imports from Britain, Germany, Belgium, Mexico and Ireland. Foreign brands brewed under licence in Greece are Amstel, Kaiser Heineken and Fischer. Popular Greek labels

NON-ALCOHOLIC DRINKS

Hot coffee *(kafés)* is served *ellinikós* or 'Greek-style', freshly brewed in copper pots and served in small cups. It will probably arrive *glykós* (sweet) or even *varý glykós* (cloyingly sweet) unless you specify *métrios* (medium) or *skétos* (without sugar). Don't drink right to the bottom – the grounds settle there. Instant coffee (called 'Nes' irrespective of brand) has made big inroads in Greece; more appetising is *frappé*, cold instant coffee whipped up in a blender with or without milk *(gála)*, refreshing on a summer's day. If you prefer proper cappuccino or espresso, numerous Italian-style coffee bars will oblige you.

Soft drinks comes in all the international varieties, while juices are usually out of cartons rather than fresh-squeezed. Bottled *(enfialoméno)* still mineral water is typically from Crete or the Greek mainland mountains.

include Alfa, Mythos, Fix and Vergina (the last two the best, especially Vergina Red Lager). There are also numerous micro-breweries, though none on the islands in this guide. Brinks (Crete) or any beer from Santoríni are reliably good.

USEFUL EXPRESSIONS

Could we order, please? **Na parangiloúme, parakaló?**

I'm a vegetarian **Íme hortofágos**

The bill, please **To logariazmó, parakaló**

Enjoy the next courses (literally, 'Good continuation!')
    Kalí synéhia!

plate **piáto**	salt **aláti**
cutlery **maheropírouna**	black pepper **mávro pipéri**
glass **potíri**	Cheers! **Giámas!**
bread **psomí**	Bon appetit! **Kalí órexi!**

MENU READER

fried **tiganitó**	goat **katsíki**
baked **sto foúrno**	chicken **kotópoulo**
roasted **psitó**	lamb **arní**
grilled **sta kárvouna**	salad **saláta**
meat sautée **tianiá**	olives **eliés**
stuffed **gemistá**	wild greens **hórta**
fish **psári**	runner beans **fasolákia**
small shrimp **garídes**	aubergines/eggplants
octopus **(o)khtapódi**	**melitzánes**
swordfish **xifías**	chickpeas **revýthia**
cuttlefish **soupiá**	potatoes **patátes**
deep-water squid **thrápsalo**	rice **rýzi, piláfi**
meat **kréas**	wine **krasí**
meatballs **keftedákia**	beer **býra**
beef **moskhári, vodinó**	(chilled) water **(pagoméno)**
pork **hirinó**	**neró**

PLACES TO EAT

Price categories reflect the cost of a meal per person with modest drink intake. Except where suggested, reservations are not necessary (or even possible) – one waits, or an extra table is fitted in. Unless otherwise stated, tavernas are open daily for lunch and dinner, early May–late Oct. Payment by cash unless 'Credit cards' indicated.

€€€€ = 33–43 euros   **€€€** = 26–33 euros
€€ = 19–26 euros   **€** = below 19 euros

KOS TOWN AND SUBURBS

Ambavris € *Ambávris hamlet, 800m/yards south of Casa Romana, tel: 22420 25696.* Well-loved farmhouse-courtyard taverna. Choose a *mezédes* medley which might include lamb meatballs in ouzo sauce, husked beans with garlic, snails, *pinigoúri*, *pikhtí*, spicy *loukánika*, *fáva* purée and stuffed *anthí*. Affordably priced bottled or bulk ouzo and *tsípouro*. Dinner only May–early Oct.

Barbouni €€€€ *Georgíou Avérof 26, tel: 22420 20170.* Classier-than-normal waterside seafood spot gazing across to Turkey. All usual fishy suspects plus novelties like risotto with cuttlefish and its ink, shellfish linguini in dilled white sauce, spinach salad with pine nuts and *krasotýri*, plus a surprisingly full dessert list. Thanks to Turkish clientele, some *rakı* labels. Credit cards.

Degli Amici (Tony's) €€–€€€ *Vasiléos Georgíou 22, tel: 22420 26568.* Genuine Italian trattoria with sea views (across traffic) doing pasta, mussel and meat dishes, plus pizzas. Italian desserts (panna cotta, tiramisu) to order, grappa or limoncello as *kérazma*; bulk rosé palatable if expensive. Service copes well with crowds, but booking advisable. Credit cards.

Koako €€ *Vasiléos Georgíou 8, tel: 22420 25645.* A seafront favourite good for *magirevtá*, stuffed *anthí* and seasonal fish like *koliós* or *gávros*. Prices reflect the prime location but portions also big, quality high, and ordering bulk wine (rosé is okay) pushes down bill totals. Lunch and dinner Apr–Nov.

Mavromatis €€ *Georgíou Papandréou, start of Psalídi, tel: 22420 22433.* Venerable seaside eatery with beach loungers, and staple dishes like grilled mackerel, *moussakás* and a rocket-parmesan salad that isn't (as elsewhere) mostly lettuce. Tourist tastes mean you'll have to specifically ask for real, hand-cut chips and not packaged frozen ones. Lunch and dinner, most of the year.

Pote tin Kyriaki € *Pisándrou 9, Old Town, tel: 22420 48460 or 6930 352099.* This *mezedopolío's* signature platters include *marathópita* (fennel pie), stuffed *anthí*, mushroom sautée with vegies, *kavourdistí* (pork fry up) and assorted seafood at encouraging prices, complemented by proprietress Stamatia's strong *tsikoudiá*, and a soundtrack of Greek music for Greeks. Booking needed after 9pm. Open dinner only late May–Oct Mon–Sat, Nov–mid-May Fri–Sat.

Votsalakia €–€€ *Georgíou Avérof 10, tel: 22420 26555.* The locals' favourite seafood taverna, thanks to fair fish prices, cheery seating indoors or out according to weather, non-cheesy soundtrack and friendly staff. Do try the grilled cuttlefish and wild *hórta*. Open daily lunch and dinner except mid-Dec–mid-Jan.

AROUND THE ISLAND

Ambeli €–€€ *2.5km east of Tingáki beachfront crossroads, towards Lámbi, tel: 22420 69682.* Rural taverna where you might skip mains and choose starters like *pikhtí, yaprákia, bekrí mezé* and crispy medallion-cut chips, washed down with draught beer or wine from the surrounding vineyard (*ambéli*). Portions are big, don't over-order. May-Oct daily; Nov-April weekends.

Esperos €€ *waterfront, east from shore junction, Tingáki, tel: 22420 69753.* Better-than-average resort taverna with the usual grills and *magirevtá*, pizzas and island wine; token Thai and Indian dishes are ersatz, and avoidable. Friendly service, and free beach sunbeds over the road. Open all year (winter weekends only).

Gin's Place €–€€ *corner Kerámou & Attálou, Plataní, tel: 22420 25166.* The most casserole-orientated of four Kos-Turk tavernas here, with chickpeas, *bámies* (okra), *yaprákia*, stewed pork (obviously not strict Muslims here), and *glóssa* (sole) *plakí* amongst offerings. Fare can be a bit salty; good bulk rosé wine from Crete, the land of proprietor Rasim's ancestors. Lunch and dinner, all year.

Hasan € *Central junction, Platáni village. tel: 22420 20230.* New on the scene of Platáni tavernas, it is now reckoned the best, without Anatolian-style *mezédes* but serving creditable Adana kebab, generous okra stew, grilled vegies in yoghurt and a full drinks list, including good bulk red from the Peloponnese. Open all year (weekends only in winter).

Limiónas €€ *Limiónas cove, tel: 6932 422002.* Classic, isolated fish taverna that has elevated prices for small-portioned starters and scaly fish, but food is still tasty and (it's claimed) all non-frozen. The view encompasses Kálymnos, Psérimos and the coast from Mástihari southwest.

Magic Beach €–€€ *tel: 22420 71894 or 6944782789.* The most accomplished and friendliest of the snack bars/tavernas above the southwesterly beaches. The terrace, allowing sweeping views across to Nísyros and Tílos islands, is lapped by junipers at the top of the sand dunes. Prices reflect the remoteness and local monopoly. Starters include well-done *kolokythokeftédes* and *khtapódi xydáto.*

Makis €€ *One lane inland, Mastihari, tel: 22420 59061.* Whilst unpromising looking, this has always been one of the island's best seafood tavernas. Outermost tables catch the breeze and permit oblique sea views, but fresh-off-the-boat (if starkly presented) fish and seafood remain the chief attraction, with token salads and dips preceding. Open all day, all year.

Neromylos/Watermill € *Platía Karydiás, Ziá, tel: 6972 292109.* Dusk is the time to sit under *Neromylos'* giant walnut tree and savour a drink (perhaps house lemonade), or cake with ice cream. Also crêpes, fruit salad, sandwiches and a short cocktail list. This is the site of the last intact watermill on Kos, which ground grain until the 1960s. Open 10am–evening Apr–Nov.

Oromedon €€ *Ziá access road. tel: 22420 69983.* Come here after climbing Hristós to watch the famous sunset, while savouring *hortópita* (greens pie), *yaprákia*, *keftedákia* and good bread; there are roast-goat or -pork mains for bigger appetites, and grilled vegies or mushrooms in balsamic vinegar for vegetarian palates. Lunch and dinner, late Apr–late Oct.

Old Pyli €€ *Paleó Pylí access road, Amanioú village, tel: 22420 41659.* Giorgos, originally a Mastihári fisherman, keeps this taverna below the ruins of medieval Pylí. He serves his son's daily catch, plus vegetarian starters, wood-oven-baked bread and his own wine (a bit heavy). Unbeatable terrace views.

Palia Pigi € *Pigí district, Pylí village, tel: 22420 41510.* Basic but honest fare (*loukánika*, caper salad, *biftékia*, marinated octopus, *pikhtí*, *anthí*, *bakaliáros*, beets) at this taverna tucked away under a giant ficus, beside a cistern fountain with lion-headed spouts amidst a bird-filled oasis. Lunch and dinner, late March–Nov.

Plori €€ *100m/yards west of shore plaza along beach promenade, Tingáki, tel: 22420 69686.* A good selection of *mezédes* like tangy *krasotýri*, lamb-and-liver *tigania* and aubergine mash; also standard mains for bigger appetites. Good beer and wine selection, oddly sparse ouzo list. Both Greeks and foreigners attend. Lunch and dinner all year (winter weekends only).

Teos €€ *Seafront, Kardámena, tel: 22420 92034 or 6988 145692.* Kardámena's go-to seafood place; their own trawler brings in the daily catch, with keen per-kilo prices. Both fried-courgette starter and *sargós* (white bream) were perfect, the fish appearing with an appreciable side-salad and chips. Good Cretan bulk wine. By Kardámena standards, it's ancient (founded 1984), and tellingly the only local taverna open in winter. Lunch and dinner all year (may shut weekdays in winter).

NÍSYROS

Astradeni €€ *Pálli waterfront, tel: 22420 31061.* Despite being opposite the yacht mooring (often a kiss of death), *Astradeni* has reasonable per-kilo prices for perfectly grilled fish, a limited range of starters (including the best *melitzanosaláta* on Nísyros) and lovely chips – a normal portion will feed three. Friendly service, well-priced beer and wine.

Bacareto Margarita €€ *Lekandió seafront Mandráki, tel: 22420 31842.* Despite the name, chef Davide Sacco purveys a repertoire of Venetian meat or seafood dishes, every imaginable pasta recipe, gnocchi, a range of salads, creative Greek *mezédes*, and (in high season) Italian desserts. Dinner only, May–Oct.

Balkoni tou Emboriou € *Emboriós central plaza, tel: 22420 31607.* Always packed for the sake of *keftédes*, beets with greens, capers, *lahanodolmádes*, baked swordfish with vegetables, *pittiá* (vegetable risolles) and (by night) grills – and for the view over the volcanic zone.

Limenari € *eponymous cove west of Pálli, tel: 22420 31023.* This secluded taverna, in a terraced valley, captures many local diners thanks to fair prices and portions for caper-topped salads, fish, a few dishes of the day like *papoutsáki*, and made-to-order *tyrokafterí* (which takes time to arrive; service generally lags). Islanders and army conscripts go all year.

KÁLYMNOS AND TÉLENDOS

Georgios Mamouzelos €€ *Linária promenade, 22430 47809.* The best seaside taverna on this coast, featuring swordfish with impeccable medallion chips, stuffed peppers with balsamic vinegar, superior lamb chops and fried aubergines covered with grated parmesan. You'll reserve a table or wait for one, and tolerate often erratic service.

Kafenes € *Platía Hristoú, Póthia, tel: 22430 28727.* Working since 1950, this hole-in-the-wall purveys generous platters like crunchy *maridáki*, exceptionally tender *khtapodokeftédes* (octopus rissoles), local cheese or mountainous salads fit for two; try the 'green' with purslane, rocket, sun-dried tomato and lots of parmesan. Expect to wait for a table after dark. Lunch and dinner year round.

Plaka € *East shore promenade, 200m/yards north of jetty, Télendos, tel: 22430 47921.* The only shoreline taverna here that doesn't tout;

they don't have to, with very fair prices for tasty fresh tuna, swordfish, wild sea-bass, some meat dishes and typical salads or starters. Beer, ouzo or bulk wine to drink.

Stukas €–€€ *Yacht marina, Póthia, tel: 6970 802346 or 6957 406977.* A good all-rounder with big portions, pleasant service and traffic-free waterside tables. Pork *kopsídia* (round-bone chops), a starter and a beer falls in the first price category; ordering seafood pushes bills up a notch. Lunch and dinner, all year.

LÉROS

Dimitris O Karaflas €–€€ *Spiliá district, off the Pandéli-Vromólithos road, tel: 22470 25626 or 6977 080599.* Some of the heartiest food on Léros, and knockout views of Vromólithos. Standouts include *kremmydópita* (onion pie), smoked mackerel, roast pork *kotsí* (shank) and heaping salads. Open all year, lunch and dinner.

O Mylos €€€–€€€€ *Beside sea-marooned windmill, Agía Marína, tel: 22470 24894.* *Mezédes* include *garidopílafo* (shrimp rice) and *kolokythokeftédes* (courgette patties). Best order simple mains like grilled fish – 'seafood' *makaronáda* consisted of precisely four prawns atop a pile of spaghetti drenched in inedible sauce. Minus points for exorbitantly priced ouzo; decent Lafazanis bulk rosé is contrastingly affordable. Open lunch and dinner late Mar–late Oct; reservations mandatory July–Aug, when Turkish yachties crowd Léros's most romantic setting. Credit cards.

Paradisos €€–€€€ *Vromólithos beach, tel: 22470 24632.* Best for *mezédes* and light platters like crispy *atherína* (sand smelt), beets, superior *melitzanosaláta*, *hórta* or big salads. Broad range of beers, and premium Greek wine list. Ordering proper mains entails the higher price category. Try for a sea-view terrace table, and afterwards one of the sunbeds on the beach just below.

To Steki tou Dimitri € *far north end of Álinda, tel: 22470 22413.* Superior *mezédes* like *kolokythokeftédes* and aubergine roulade baked with cheese and bacon. Cheap but cheerful *hýma* white wine, friendly service too. You need to reserve Thursday and Saturday nights when there's live music, or for a table on the sand next to the tiny anchorage here.

PÁTMOS

Hiliomodi € *just of the Hóra road, Skála, tel: 22470 34179.* This 1980s-founded seafood *ouzerí* has benefitted from changed management. Expect a drawerful of scaly fish like black bream, and starters like *taramosaláta* and *stiforádiko,* a springtime *hórta.* Good *hýma* wine from the Peloponnese, seating in the charming alley behind or up on the roof terrace. April—end Nov, 6pm—midnight.

Ktima Petra €€ *Pétra beach, south of Gríkou, tel: 22470 33207.* Chunky *melitzanosaláta,* brown bread to scoop it with, lush rocket salad, own-made *yaprákia* and pork *giouvétsi* are typical lunchtime offerings, with grills too after dark; most ingredients are from their own *ktíma* (farm). Excellent *retsína* from Thebes. Some patrons take a dip of the pebble beach while waiting for orders. Lunch and dinner Apr—late Sept, lunch only early Oct. Summer reservations advisable.

Lambi €–€€ *Lámbi beach, north end of island, tel: 22470 31490.* Another reliable beach taverna, since 1958; simple presentation for top ingredients. Try the faultlessly grilled fresh squid served with delicious chips. Some tables set out on the famous pebbles. Open noon until sunset, Easter Weds–Oct.

Panagos tou Sarandi € *central junction, Kámbos village, tel: 22470 31570.* A beacon of *magirevtá* such as baked *palamídi* (north Aegean tuna), chickpea hotpot or *soupióryzo* (cuttlefish-rice), plus good bulk wine. A museum's worth of old photos inside; some outdoor seating. Lunch and dinner, all year.

Tzivaeri €€ *behind Theológos town beach, by car park, Skála, tel: 22470 31170.* Durable upstairs ouzerí with all standard platters present and more than correct, including yaprákia, tangy tyrokafterí, succulent grilled *plevrótous* and snails in rosemary. Good *hýma* wine, pricey ouzo. Much sought-after summer terrace, tasteful interior for cooler months; live Greek music Fri or Sat (reservations needed). Dinner daily, May–Oct; weekends only Nov–April.

A–Z TRAVEL TIPS

A Summary of Practical Information

A

ACCOMMODATION

Hotels. Hotels are classified from five stars down to zero. Ratings are dictated primarily by the common facilities at the hotel, not room quality, so a particular three-star room may be just as comfortable as a nearby five-star room, but the hotel itself may lack an events hall, swimming pool, spa or multiple restaurants on the premises.

Many hotels on Kos have contracts with European tour operators. This means that in peak season it may be difficult to find desirable accommodation. If you intend to arrive between late June and early September it is wise to book in advance. At the beginning and end of the season (April–mid-June and October) it is easier to get a good deal direct or through a booking site. Most hotels away from Kos Town, on Nísyros, and on Pátmos close from November to March. Interestingly, Léros has two comfortable hotels working year round, and some hotels on Kálymnos stay open during winter for rock-climbers. In peak season there may be a surcharge if you stay less than four days, or an absolute minimum stay.

One thing to beware of is the proliferation on Kos of mandatorily all-inclusive resorts. While notionally attractive to families, they seldom offer great value or great taste. We do not list any exclusively all-inclusive accommodation; however some of our listings do offer this as an option.

***Domátia* and apartments.** *Enikiazómena domátia* (rented rooms) or full-sized apartments *(diamerísmata)* exist, especially behind the better beaches. Both licensed rooms and apartments are rated by the tourism authorities at from one to three 'keys' based on facilities. Arrivals by ferry or catamaran at Kos Harbour or Skála on Pátmos may be besieged by placard-waving accommodation touts; it is unwise to follow them, as only proprietors of substandard or unlicensed lodgings resort to this tactic, and you will probably choose to move the next morning.

AIRPORTS

Kos' international airport (IATA code KGS, tel: 22420 56000) lies towards the southwest tip of the island, 24km (15 miles) from Kos Town. Its website (www.kos-airport.com) furnishes real-time arrival and departure information. One of the older Greek-island airports, it has scarcely changed since opening in 1964 and expanding in 1980, and is grossly inadequate for the current traffic in season. Chances for another makeover in the prevailing economic climate are slim. If your flight is delayed, there's a pleasant snack bar just outside the airport grounds at the edge of Andimáhia village, plainly visible across the car park.

Between April and Oct, five times daily from 7.55am to 5.20pm (with one later service Tue, Thu, Sat), there is bus service (€3.20) into Kos Town, via Mastihári. During June to September, this increases to ten daily Mon–Sat 8am–11pm, but just three 9am–5pm on Sun. A taxi to Kos Town or Psalídi will cost €35–40 depending on time of day, number of bags and exact destination.

Kálymnos and Léros also have airports (taxi access only), currently receiving flights solely from Athens and nearby islands. The Kálymnos runway is set to be expanded to allow direct flights from overseas in future.

B

BICYCLE AND SCOOTER HIRE

Kos is one of the few Greek municipalities which actively caters to cylists. Psalídi is linked with Lámbi by a popular bike lane, though going through Kos Town itself there are hazardous discontinuities around the inner harbour. Beyond Lámbi or the edge of Kos Town, smart cyclists use the back-roads to get to Tingáki and Marmári, not the lethal main island trunk-road. There are so many agencies renting pedal-bikes on Kos that you practically trip over them. Rates range from €5 per day for the most basic, five-gear boneshaker to €20 for a top-end, multi-speed mountain bike.

Hiring a small motorbike is popular for cruising the resorts and immediate environs; rates are €15–18 per day for a 50cc machine, lower for three days or more. However, they're not really suitable for covering long distances on Kos, and every year sees serious injuries and fatalities involving riders.

It is illegal in Greece to drive any scooter – even a 50cc one – without a full A1 or A category motorcycle licence (British license categories AM, p and Q with scooter entitlement are not recognised), though many agencies ignore this law. If you hire a two-wheeler without the appropriate licence, any insurance you have will be void if you are injured or involved in an accident. Agencies may offer you a quad bike as an alternative, at somewhere between the rental cost of a scooter or a car. They are slow and actually less safe than a two-wheeler – thus helmets are issued; the Greek slang for them (*gouroúnia*, or swine) is indicative of their low status.

All riders must wear helmets (stiff fines for non-compliance; agencies offer wonky ones) and should proceed with caution, particularly where sand or gravel make road surfaces slippery.

BUDGETING FOR YOUR TRIP

Kos and neighbouring islands are moderately expensive destinations by European standards.

Flight Athens–Kos: €70–160 (one-way by season).

Boat ticket Athens–Kos: €56 (one-way, deck class) to €79 (one-way, cheapest cabin).

Day trip to Nísyros: €24 from Kardámena, €30 from Kos Town

Mid-range hotel: €55–100 (one night for two).

Mid-range restaurant: €22–35 (full meal for one).

Luxury hotel: €100–210 (one night for two)

Admission charges: €2–5 (museums and archaeological sites).

Car rental: €30 per day on Kos, €190 per week (small car in peak season, walk-in rate).

Litre of fuel, diesel/normal/super €1.25/1.60/1.90
Bus fare: ticket prices range from €2–4.40 on Kos, less on Pátmos or Kálymnos.

C

CAR RENTAL (see also Driving)

Advance booking online typically results in savings of up to half off of walk-in rates. Recommended aggregator sites include www.comparecarrentals.co.uk, www.rentalcargroup.com and www.cardelmar.com.

Reputable local agencies give reasonable service and keener pricing than major international chains. Two recommended ones in Kos Town are Safari, corner Harmýlou and Karaiskáki, tel: 22420 21023, www.safari-rentacar.gr, and Autoway, Vassiléos Georgíou 18, tel: 22420 25326, www.autowaykos.gr; on Kálymnos, we suggest Auto Market in Póthia (tel: 22430 24202, www.kalymnoscars.gr).

A national driving licence, held for at least one year, driver age over 21, is accepted for EU/EEA nationals. Other nationals must carry an International Driving Permit in addition to their home licence. You will also need a credit card to avoid paying a large cash deposit.

Quoted rates should include VAT and CDW (Collision Damage Waiver). However, all agencies have a waiver excess of between €400 and €800 – the amount you are responsible for if you smash a vehicle, even with CDW coverage. It is strongly suggested you purchase extra cover (often called Waiver Excess Insurance) to nullify this risk. Daily rates offered by agencies themselves are expensive; it's far more advantageous to get a waiver excess policy in advance – by the year or by the day – through specialists like www.insurance4carhire.com or www.carhireexcess.com.

CLIMATE

Global climate change makes generalising about Aegean weather unwise, but you still stand an excellent chance of blue, rain-free skies between late May and mid-October. Midday temperatures may reach a sweltering 38ºC (101ºF) during summer, with warm nights, although evenings are cooler early and late in the season when daily highs are about 30° C (86° F).

The northerly *meltémi* wind buffets the northwest coast of Kos, cooling it significantly all season. Kálymnos, Léros and Pátmos can also be very breezy, though Pátmos' east coast (where most beaches are) is relatively calm.

The first autumn storm usually hits late September or early October, but serious rain does not commence until December, falling intermittently until May. Winter outdoors can be very pleasant but the sea is too cold for most bathers until late April.

CLOTHING

In summer you require little clothing. Cotton shorts or lightweight trousers and T-shirts or lightweight dresses are fine for sightseeing. Bring comfortable shoes for archaeological sites, plus a hat and sunglasses. If you have forgotten anything, boutiques in Kos Town and Póthia are well stocked (if not remarkably cheap outside sale periods).

When visiting churches or monasteries, both men and women should cover their shoulders; men should wear long trousers, and women a skirt that covers their knees.

Very few tavernas have a dress code, although smarter hotels require long trousers for men at dinner. A light wrap or jacket is useful for evenings in early or late season, while a wind-cheater is good for the decks of excursion boats or catamarans.

CRIME AND SAFETY

Kos and neighbours rate relatively well both in terms of personal safety and the security of belongings. But it is still prudent to lock valuables in your room safe, and not to leave phones, tablets, etc. unsupervised on the beach or even in a locked rental car – break-ins are increasing. Don't accept rides from strangers when returning late from clubbing, and always use official taxis.

If you do fall victim to crime, contact the ordinary local police – insurance claim forms will not be valid without their report.

All obvious recreational drugs are illegal in Greece, and those arrested on narcotics charges can spend up to 18 months on remand before charges are filed. If you take any prescription painkiller or tranquilliser, carry your supply in the original pharmacy container.

D

DRIVING

Road conditions. Kos main roads are mostly paved but still dangerous, especially the main trunk road between Kos Town and Kéfalos, too narrow for its traffic load and venue for many accidents. Local driving habits leave much to be desired; favourite tricks to watch for include barging out of side roads without looking, overtaking on one's right, and oncoming vehicles driving in the centre of the pavement. Most of Kos can be visited by normal rental car, though a few remote beaches are best approached by jeep. Adjacent islands present no special road problems.

Signage, and advance notice for turnings, is acceptable at best. Since many place-names have been transliterated idiosyncratically into Roman lettering and signposted at different times, you may find

Are we on the right road for...? **Páma kalá giá...?**
Full tank, please. **Óso pérni, parakaló.**
super/lead-free/diesel **soúper/amólyvdis/dízel**
Check the oil/tires/battery. **Na elénxete ta ládia/ta lástiha/ti bataría.**
My car has broken down. **I amáxi mou éhi páthi vlávi.**
There's been an accident. **Égine éna atýhima.**

the same village name or attraction written different ways, only one rendition agreeing with your map. Similarly, distances may yo-yo up and down as signs do not keep pace with road-straightening works.

Brown signs with yellow lettering indicate an archaeological site or other monument – not all of them are must-sees.

Rules and regulations. Traffic drives on the right and passes on the left, yielding to vehicles from the right except at roundabouts where one supposedly yields to the left (often countermanded by confusing stop-or-yield-sign schemes). Speed limits on open roads are 90km/h (55mph) and in towns 50km/h (30mph) unless otherwise stated, although most locals ignore these. Speed-limit and distance signs are in kilometres.

Seat-belt use is compulsory (€175 fine for non-use), as are helmets when riding any two-wheeler (identical fine for non-compliance). Drink-driving laws are strict – expect fines of €400–700 and licence loss if caught – and breathalyser checkpoints proliferate at night and weekends. All cars must carry a reflective warning triangle, a fire extinguisher and a first-aid kit; some rental companies skimp on these. Fines must be paid within ten calendar days at a post office, with proof of payment taken to the designated police station, where your licence may be held to ransom meanwhile.

Kos Town and Póthia are full of one-way systems, which many scooter-riders (and some car-drivers) disregard. Many – especially young conscripts driving army trucks – are inexperienced and may not be insured. Give them a wide berth. Pedestrians often step out into the roadway without looking.

Parking space is tightly controlled and hard to find in the business districts of both Kos Town and Póthia. Rather than try to decipher posted rules or find tickets, just park free in the residential districts and walk into the centre. Parking along Kos harbour quay is banned except along one wall of the castle. In Skála Pátmos, it is prudent to use the free public car park behind Theológos beach.

Breakdowns and accidents. If you have an accident or breakdown, put a red warning triangle some distance behind you to warn on-coming traffic, then ring your rental office. They will probably come out to you themselves rather than summoning one of the emergency roadside services.

If an accident involves another vehicle, do not admit fault or move either car until the police come out and prepare a report; a copy will be given to you to present to the rental agency. It is an offence to leave the scene of an accident, or move either vehicle before this has been done.

Road signs. Most road signs are the standard pictographs used throughout Europe but you may also see some of these written signs:

Detour **ΠΑΡΑΚΑΨΗ/Parákampsi**
Parking **ΠΑΡΚΙΓΚ/Párking**
Forbidden **...ΑΠΑΓΟΡΕΥΕΤΑΙ/...apagorévete**
Be careful **ΠΡΟΣΟΧΗ/Prosohí**
Stop **ΣΤΑΜΑΤΑ/Stamáta**
For pedestrians **ΓΙΑ ΠΕΖΟΥΣ/Gia pezoús**
Danger **ΚΙΝΔΙΝΟΣ/Kíndinos**
No entry **ΑΠΑΓΟΡΕΥΕΤΑΙ Η ΕΙΣΟΔΟΣ/Apagorévete i ísodos**

E

ELECTRICITY

Electrical current is 220–240 volts/50 cycles. Plugs are of the Continental two-prong type. Adaptor plugs are available, but it is best to buy one before you leave home – UK-to-Continental are much harder to find than North-American-to-Continental.

an adapter **énas prosarmostís**

EMBASSIES AND CONSULATES

There are no consulates of any English-speaking country on the islands in this guide. All national embassies are located in Athens.

Australian Embassy & Consulate: Corner Kifissías and Alexándras avenues, Level 6, Thon Building, 115 23 Ambelókipi; tel: 210 87 04 000, http://greece.embassy.gov.au/athn/home.html

British Embassy & Consulate: Ploutárhou 1, 106 75 Athens; tel: 210 72 72 600, http://ukingreece.fco.gov.uk/en.

Canadian Embassy: Ethnikís Andistáseos 48, 152 31 Halándri; tel: 210 72 73 400, www.canadainternational.gc.ca/greece-grece

Irish Embassy: Vassiléos Konstandínou 7, 106 74 Athens; tel: 210 72 32 771, www.dfa.ie/irish-embassy/greece/.

South African Embassy & Consulate Kifissías 60, 151 25 Maroússi; tel 210 61 78 020.

US Embassy & Consulate: Vassilísis Sofías 91, 115 21 Athens; tel: 210 72 12 951, http://athens.usembassy.gov.

EMERGENCIES

The following emergency numbers are valid on the islands.

Police: 100
Ambulance: 166
Fire: 199
Coast guard: 108
Forest fire reporting: 191

G

GAY AND LESBIAN TRAVELLERS

Greece has historically been a very conservative country where traditional family relationships are a core value. However, the wide variety of international tourists arriving on Kos means that gay and lesbian visitors are taken in stride. That said, there are no exclusively, or predominantly, gay clubs or beaches.

GETTING THERE

By air. Direct scheduled services from Britain, between March and October, include easyJet (www.easyjet.com) from Gatwick and Glasgow; Jet2 (www.jet2.com) from East Midlands, Leeds/Bradford and Manchester; and Ryanair (www.ryanair.com) from Liverpool and London Stansted. British Airways (www.britishairways.com) arrives from Heathrow Tuesday and Saturday from early May to late September.

From North America, you must reach Athens first and then continue for another 50min on the sole airline on the domestic route: Aegean (www.aegeanair.com). Flights fill quickly in summer – even business sells out – and must be booked well in advance. Check the competition, Astra (www.astra-airlines.gr), to see if they have begun flying in from Athens; they already do from Thessaloníki.

From the UK, Aegean and BA provide scheduled full-service flights to Athens. Direct flights from North America to Athens are provided only by Delta Airlines (www.delta.com) from JFK, and seasonally from Philadelphia by US Airways (www.usairways.com).

From Australia and New Zealand there are only indirect flights; the most reliable providers are Etihad Airways (www.etihadairways.com), Qatar Airways (www.qatarairways.com) and Emirates (www.emirates.com).

By boat. Kos is connected to Piraeus, Athens' main port, by three to six weekly car and passenger ferries; frequency is highest during summer. Boats can be crowded at peak times – buy tickets for cars or a cabin as far in advance as possible. A good online resource for checking schedules is www.gtp.gr.

Currently just one company, Blue Star (www.bluestarferries.gr), serves this route. Journey time varies: 10.5 hours with an intervening stop only at Santoríni, 11.5 hours via Pátmos and Léros. There are also links with many other Dodecanese on the catamarans *Dodekanisos Pride* and *Dodekanisos Express* (www.12ne.gr/el/). Kálymnos and the westerly Kos port of Mastihári are linked two or three times daily by ro-ro ferry (www.anemferries.gr/en/timetable/).

GUIDES AND TOURS

On nearby Rhodes, Triton Holidays (Plastíra 9, Rhodes Town; tel: 22410 21690; www.tritondmc.gr) can arrange discounted quality accommodation on Nísyros, Kálymnos, Léros and Pátmos, plus all necessary transfers between islands.

H

HEALTH AND MEDICAL CARE

Emergency treatment is given free at state hospital casualty wards (ask for the *thálamo epigón peristatiká*) to EU residents, who must carry a European Health Insurance Card, obtainable in the UK online at www.ehic.org.uk.

Kos' state hospital is in town on Venizélou, just south of the ancient agora. But public health provision is in free-fall across Greece, with dire shortages of medicines and material, so if you are privately insured, go instead directly opposite to Kos Medicare at no. 5 (tel: 22420 23330, www.kosmedicare.gr), with a branch in Kardámena (tel: 22420 92770), plus their own ambulance which can be summoned 24hr. There are also state hospitals on Kálymnos and Léros, but only rural clinics on Nísyros and Pátmos.

If you have a minor problem, look for a pharmacy *(farmakío)*, identified by a green cross; most pharmacists speak some English. Pharmacies open Mon–Fri 8am–2pm; outside of these hours only duty pharmacies operate. A roster of the day's after-hours pharmacies should be posted on the door of each pharmacy.

Mosquitoes can be a nuisance all season. Topical repellent is useful from dusk onwards; accommodation proprietors often provide insecticide tablets vaporised by a plug-in device. Spiny sea urchins on submerged rocks can injure inattentive swimmers. Avoidance is the best tactic, but failing that, dig out the spine tips with a sterilised sewing needle and olive oil.

The Greek sun is strong; limit your exposure time, apply sunblock (SPF 30+) regularly and use a hat. Children's skin should be especially well protected.

Kos tap water is safe to drink, and the central mountain has two popular, potable springs; Póthia (Kálymnos) has street-corner, purified-water machines to fill bottles, some free, some coin-op; Pátmos has excellent artesian water, on tap at Skála marina and at Kámbos. Otherwise, bottled water is universally available. Always carry water to the beach or when sightseeing to prevent dehydration.

L

LANGUAGE

The sounds of the Greek language do not always correspond to exact equivalents in English, and some letters of the Greek alphabet do not have a precise match in the Roman alphabet. This explains inconsistent spellings on road signs – for example, *ágios* may be spelled *ághios* and *áyios* in the Roman alphabet, although it is always pronounced the same. Accentuation is also essential when pronouncing Greek. Throughout this book we have accented vowels within each word to show which syllable to stress, except for one-syllable words.

People working anywhere near the tourist industry will have a basic English vocabulary, and many speak English very well.

The table below lists the 24 letters of the Greek alphabet in their upper- and lower-case forms, followed by the closest individual or combined letters to which they correspond in English.

Α	α	a	as in father
Β	β	v	as in English
Γ	γ	g	as in go (except pronounced 'y' before 'e' and 'i' sounds)
Δ	δ	d	like th in this

E	ε	e	as in get
Z	ζ	z	as in English
H	η	i	as in ski
Θ	θ	th	like th in thin
I	ι	i	as in ski
K	κ	k	as in English
Λ	λ	l	as in English
M	μ	m	as in English
N	ν	n	as in English
Ξ	ξ	x	as in box
O	ο	o	as in toad
Π	π	p	as in English
P	ρ	r	as in English
Σ	σ/ς	s	as in English, except sounds like z before m or g sounds
T	τ	t	as in English
Y	υ	y	as in country
Φ	φ	f	as in English
X	χ	h	as in Scottish loch
Ψ	ψ	ps	as in tipsy
Ω	ω	o	as in bone
AI	αι	e	as in *hay*
AY	αυ	av	as in *avant-garde*
EI	ει	i	as in *ski*
EY	ευ	ev	as in *ever*
OI	οι	i	as in *ski*
OY	ου	ou	as in *soup*
ΓΓ	γγ	ng	as in *longer*
ΓK	γκ	g	as in *gone*
ΓΞ	γξ	nx	as in *anxious*
ΜΠ	μπ	b or mb	as in *beg* or *compass*
NT	ντ	d or nd	as in *dog* or *under*

MAPS

You'll find free advertiser maps at hotels, Kos airport and car-rental offices, adequate for Kos Town only. The sole maps of Kos and the surrounding islands worth buying are produced by Terrain (www.terrainmaps.gr; all islands in this guide at scales 1:20,000–1:45,000) or Anavasi (www.anavasi.gr; Kos, Kálymnos, Pátmos, scales 1:20,000–1:60,000). They are only sporadically available on the islands concerned, so ideally obtain them in advance.

MEDIA

Newspapers. You will be able to buy all major European newspapers at resort newsagents. A reliable outlet in Kos Town is News-stand, just off Platía Eleftherías on Ríga Fereoú.

Television. Most hotels of three stars and above have a range of satellite channels, including CNN and BBC World. The Greek state channel ET1 often has foreign films in the original language after 10pm.

MONEY

Currency. For the moment, Greece still uses the euro (abbreviated €), with notes of 5, 10, 20, 50, 100, 200, 100 and 500 euros; each euro comprises 100 cents and coins have denominations of 1, 2, 5, 10, 20 and 50 cents plus 1 and 2 euros.

Currency exchange. Most banks and some agents exchange foreign notes, but commissions are comparable to ATMs (see below) and queues long, so preferably obtain cash from an ATM. Exchange rates, the same everywhere, are usually posted on a digital notice-board inside the bank or in the window.

Travellers cheques: Not recommended – expect severe delays or outright refusals in banks or travel agencies.

ATMs. All resort areas, and larger inland settlements, have at least one ATM, accepting most debit or credit cards. Despite commissions levied by your home bank, this is the most convenient and quickest way to get cash – although machines may run out of notes at weekends. If given an option, always take euros at your own bank's exchange rate – do not let the machine do this, you will lose about 3 percent more.

Credit cards. Many hotels, restaurants, filling stations, travel agencies and shops accept credit cards, but as many do not. Some collect 3–5 percent extra for credit card payments, to cover bank charges.

I want to change some pounds/dollars. **Thélo na alláxo merikés líres/meriká dollária.**
How much commission do you charge? **Póso promýthia hreónete?**
Can I pay with this credit card? **Boró na pliróso me avtí tin pistotikí kárta?**

O

OPENING TIMES

Opening hours differ for official bodies and private businesses. They also vary significantly between high and low season. To be sure of service or admission, appear between 9am and 1pm, Tues–Fri.

State museums work Tue–Sun 8.30am–3pm; private ones vary. Most archaeological sites are open continuously until 8pm during summer but close much earlier in winter. Last admissions are 20–30 minutes before the official closing time; we cite the last admission time in this guide.

Banks operate Mon–Thu 8am–2.30pm, Fri 8am–2pm. Smaller shops work Mon–Sat 9am–2.30pm, plus Tue, Thu and Fri 5.30pm–

8.30pm (6–9pm in midsummer); supermarkets are open year-round 7/8am–9pm Mon–Fri, 8am–7/8pm Sat. A few also open 11am–4pm on Sunday. In peak season tourist-orientated shops stay open daily until late. Filling stations work daily 8am–9pm in summer (closing 8pm otherwise); many close altogether on Sunday.

P

POLICE

Ordinary police, including traffic police *(trohéa),* wear a two-tone blue uniform. The tourist police is a special branch dealing with tourist problems and complaints. They speak English and wear dark grey uniforms.

Emergency: tel: 100
Non-emergency (Kos Town): tel: 22420 22222
Tourist police: Aktí Miaoúli 2, Kos Town, tel: 22420 26666

Where's the nearest police station? **Pou íne to kondinótero astynomikó tmíma?**

POST OFFICES

Post offices (Mon–Fri 7.30am–2.30pm) are indicated by a yellow-and-blue stylised Hermes head and the initials ELTA (EΛTA in Greek). The Kos Town and Póthia (Kálymnos) post offices are marked on our maps. Allow 4–7 days delivery time for postcards to Europe, 9–14 days for the rest of the world.

PUBLIC HOLIDAYS

Official holidays, when everything will be shut, are as follows:
1 January New Year's Day *(Protohroniá)*
6 January Epiphany *(Ágia Theofánia)*
25 March Greek Independence Day/Annunciation *(Evangelismós)*

1 May May Day *(Protomagiá)*

15 August Dormition of the Virgin *(Kímisis tis Theotókou)*

28 October 'No' or *'Ohi'* Day

25 December Christmas Day *(Hristoúgenna)*

26 December *Sýnaxis tis Panagías* (Gathering of the Virgin's Entourage)

Movable official holidays include the first day of Lent (Clean Monday; 48 days before Easter Sunday), Good Friday, Easter Monday and Pentecost (Whit Monday, *tou Agíou Pnévmatos*; 50 days after Easter Sunday).

R

RELIGION

Most islanders belong to the Greek Orthodox Church, though there is a significant Muslim minority on Kos, with three of the five mosques used regularly. Mass schedules are posted outside the one Roman Catholic church, Ámnós tou Theoú, southwest of Kos Town.

T

TELEPHONES

The international code for Greece is 30. Land-line numbers have 10 digits; the first five digits, beginning with 2, tell you which island or town the phone is in. Greek mobile numbers begin with 69 and also have 10 digits.

Card-operated telephone booths are noisy and almost extinct. Rather than use OTE (the Greek telecoms entity) calling cards, most people buy prepaid discount calling cards with free access numbers prefixed 807 (reachable from any call box or private phone) and a 12-digit PIN. Rates are similar to using Skype to a land line. Hotels levy ruinous surcharges for ordinary direct-dial calls; usually, switchboard circuitry permits use of discount cards from room phones.

Mobile users can roam on any of three local networks, and with 2015 reductions in roaming charges within the EU, both making and receiving calls, or texting, is affordable. Do not let non-EU Turkish mobile providers across the narrow straits 'grab' your number; you will have an unpleasant surprise come the next bill. Only if holidaying for more than a week might you consider buying a Greek SIM. It (and the phone) must be registered at purchase, but credit remains valid for six months from each top-up, the number for a year.

TIME ZONES

Greece is two hours ahead of Greenwich Mean Time and also observes European Daylight Saving Time – moving the clocks one hour forward at 3am on the last Sunday in March, one hour back at 3am on the last Sunday in October.

New York	London	Jo'burg	Kos	Sydney	Auckland
5am	10am	11am	**noon**	7pm	9pm

TIPPING

Service is included in restaurant and bar bills, but it is customary to leave 10 percent of the bill on the table for wait-staff.

Taxi drivers are not tipped per se except at Easter week, but collect €0.32 extra per bag in the boot, plus surcharges for entering Kos airport (€2) or any harbour (€0.80).

Hotel chambermaids should be tipped around €1 per day. Bellhops get up to €2, depending on luggage.

TOILETS

Public toilets are scarce. All museums and cafés have decent facilities. Older waste pipes in Greece are narrow and easily clogged. Never put toilet paper into the bowl – always use the bin provided.

TOURIST INFORMATION

Kos Town's tourist office (irregular hours, staff moonlights elsewhere, no phone) is indicated on our map. The Kálymnos municipal tourist office is shown on the Póthia map (Mon–Fri 8am–3pm; tel: 22430 50596).

For tourist information before you travel to Greece, contact one of the following overseas offices of the Greek National Tourism Organisation (www.visitgreece.gr):

Australia: 37–49 Pitt Street, Sydney, NSW2000; tel: (2) 9241 1663.
UK and Ireland: Portland House, 4 Great Portland Street, London W1W 8QJ tel: (020) 7495 9300.
US: 305 East 47th Street, New York, NY 10017; tel: (212) 421 5777.

TRANSPORT

Bus. Kos buses are divided into two networks: KTEL, for long-distance services (schedules at www.ktel-kos.gr, station tel: 22420 22292) to Ziá, Tingáki, Marmári, Pylí, Mastihári, Kardámena and Kéfalos, and urban buses (tel: 22420 26276) running various routes out to Psalídi, Bros Thermá, Platáni and the ancient Askli-pion. Both the KTEL station and urban-bus terminal are marked on our town map.

Kálymnos has a reasonable bus service based in Póthia, while Pátmos has a decent one with a hub in Skála. Léros and Nísyros have more rudimentary networks.

Taxis. Kos is well equipped with grey taxis. Prices to all destinations are regulated and posted outside the arrivals terminal at the airport. Minimum fare is €3.20; the basic charge structure also appears on a laminated sheet mounted on the dashboard. Meters must be set (to €1.20) at the start of each journey; '1' indicates regular fare, '2' indicates double tariff between midnight and 5am, and/or outside urban areas. Summoning a taxi by phone incurs an extra appointment charge. At Póthia, the main taxi rank is inland at Platía Kýprou (though they meet arriving seacraft). On Léros they meet arriving craft at Lakkí and Agía Marína ports; count on €13 for a transit from Lakkí to Krithóni.

Ferries and catamarans. Large ferries tend to dock at Kos between dusk and dawn headed either direction. Scarcely more expensive, and with far more user-friendly schedules, are the local catamarans *Dodekanisos Express* and *Dodekanisos Pride*, which serve all the islands in this book during daylight hours. On most islands ferries and catamarans share the same port, though on Léros ferries anchor only at Lákki, whilst catamarans might call at either Lakkí or Agía Marína.

Caiques/*kaïkia*/water taxis. On a few routes, passenger-only speedboats or traditional caiques offer regular service: Mastihári–Póthia, Mastihári–Psérimos, Kardámena–Nísyros, Myrtiés (Kálymnos)–Pandéli (Léros), Pátmos to surrounding islets. They can be fun, but definitely not on days with heavy seas.

<hr />

V

VISAS AND ENTRY REQUIREMENTS

European Union (EU) citizens may enter Greece for an unlimited length of time with a valid passport or national identity card. Nationals of the US, Canada, Australia and New Zealand can stay for 90 days within any 180-day period upon production of a valid passport; no advance visas are needed. South Africans require a Schengen Visa, applied for in advance at a Greek embassy or consulate.

Amidst the economic crisis, Greece has strict currency export limits for its own citizens. Foreigners can import or export up to €10,000 or equivalent, provided that large sums of cash are declared upon arrival.

There are no limits on duty-paid goods imported from other EU states. Arriving from a non-EU country (eg Turkey), allowances for importing duty-free goods are 200 cigarettes or 50 cigars or 250g of tobacco; 1 litre of spirits or 4 litres of wine; 250ml of cologne or 50ml of perfume.

W

WEBSITES AND INTERNET ACCESS

Here are a few genuinely useful websites pertaining to Kos and neighbouring islands:

www.kos.gr Official municipal website; has a calendar of events.

www.kalymnos-isl.gr Excellent municipal site, with good pages on diving and climbing.

www.leros.org Some ropy English to contend with, but gives a thorough flavour of Lerian landscapes, people and traditional architecture.

www.nisyros.gr Decent municipal website; parts are still under construction.

www.patmosweb.gr, www.patmos-island.com Two competing websites which together give a full picture of the island.

http://odysseus.culture.gr Official website of the Greek Ministry of Culture, covering all state museums, castles and archaeological sites; opening hours not reliable.

www.meteo.gr Semi-official weather website, with six-hourly reports from all islands in this guide except Nísyros.

www.windguru.cz Aimed at windsurfers, with reporting stations at Marmári, Psalídi, Kálymnos, Léros and Pátmos.

www.capnbarefoot.info/start Guide to the naturist beaches of the Greek islands, which often happen to be the best ones.

Most hotels have Wi-Fi zones (usually free in common areas, often charged for in rooms). Most bars, tavernas or cafés advertise free Wi-Fi access (code protected) for patrons.

RECOMMENDED HOTELS

The following recommendations for all budgets cover Kos Town, Kos island, plus all the excursion-island destinations.

Most resort hotels have different room types including suites and superior doubles, so be specific about the type of accommodation that you are booking. Air conditioning and LCD TVs are ubiquitous, free Wi-Fi nearly so (exceptions indicated).

Unless stated otherwise, establishments operate Easter/May–October. Quoted rates include taxes and service though sometimes not breakfast (€7–13 per person). Minimum stays may apply in high season.

Almost all hotels take credit cards (we indicate 'cash only' when they don't). The following price categories are for a double room or suite per night in high season. Low season rates can be half these.

€€€€€	over 250 euros
€€€€	150–250 euros
€€€	100–150 euros
€€	60–100 euros
€	below 60 euros

KOS TOWN

Afendoulis € *Evrypýlou 1, tel: 22420 25321,* www.afendoulishotel.com. Family-run travellers' hotel: cheerful brown-tiled rooms, mostly balconied, with fridges and refurbished bathrooms. The proprietors are most helpful – they can arrange port transfers – and the breakfasts (extra), served out front, are worth ordering. Popular, so booking advisable. Open late Mar–early Nov.

Kos Aktis Art €€€€ *Vasiléos Georgíou 7, tel: 22420 47200,* www.kosaktis. gr. This listed Bauhaus hotel got a designer makeover in 2005, and now always requires booking. Standard doubles and suites, in dark brown, grey, yellow and beige strokes, have unimpeded sea views and ample balconies. Bathrooms are large, lit naturally by raising roller-blinds, and sport butler sinks plus shower-tubs. Common areas comprise a sun-lit gym, patch of beach with decking, and popular waterside restaurant/bar *H2O*, also the venue for superior breakfasts including traditional *sfoungáto* omelette and bresaola. For Med fusion fare lunch or dinner, budget €35 à la carte plus drinks, though set menus €14–20 are offered. Open all year.

Kos Hotel Junior Suites €€€ *Harmýlou 2, corner Vasiléos Georgíou, tel: 22420 47100,* www.koshotel.gr. Kos Aktis Art's sister property has an all-apartment (two-room) format good for families, fitting four, with well-equipped kitchens. Sea-facing rooms are traffic-noisy from 7am onwards; not so inward-facing units. Common facilities include a big pool, competitively priced spa and huge, natural-light gym. Wi-Fi charged extra. Open all year.

Sonia €€ *Irodótou 9, entrance on Omírou, tel: 22420 28798,* www.hotel sonia.gr. Former pension completely renovated to boutique-hotel standard: parquet, veneer or wood-effect flooring, fridges, designer bathrooms with shower cabins. Room sizes (including family quads), and balcony views, vary considerably; only 13 units, so booking suggested. Breakfast served in the lawn-garden; laundry service. Sonia's son Afendoulis speaks English. Open early Mar–20 Nov.

AROUND THE ISLAND

Aqua Blu €€€€€ *Near lighthouse, Lámbi, tel: 22420 22440,* www.aqua bluhotel.gr. The only local member of the Small Luxury Hotels chain. Dark-colour accents offset the usual lighter earth tones of Greek boutique hotels. All units have coffee-making kit and quality Apivita toiletries. The 'loft' suite with brown-and-green palette, parquet flooring and combo rain shower-whirlpool tub, enjoys views to Turkey and Psérimos. The main pool laps decking and day-beds, or there's a patch of beach with sunbeds. Spa treatments are keenly priced and there's a naturally lit gym. The in-house restaurant is excellent.

Astir Odysseus €€€€ *Coast road 3km east of central plaza, Tingáki, tel: 22420 49900,* www.astirodysseuskos.gr. Family-friendly spa resort; try for units near the beach as otherwise it's a long way down to the narrow strip of sand. Some rooms and suites share semi-private pools; most look onto lawn. Junior suites (38 sq metres) represent decent value and go fast. The spa is cheerful. Half-board as default basis.

Diamond Deluxe €€€ rooms, €€€€€ suites; *Néa Alikarnasós coast road, Lámbi; tel: 22420 48835*, www.diamondhotel.gr. Stylish, adults-only 'wellness and business' hotel, whose focal features include two pools (one for laps, the other curvy), water features, and bar. Many units, in several grades, open directly onto the bigger pool, though some suites have private ones. White-plastered, stone-clad mid-range rooms have veneer flooring and marble-surfaced bathrooms. Basement spa, gym and small but deep indoor pool.

Esperia €€ *main access road, Marmári, tel: 22420 42010*, www.hotel esperiakos.gr. One of the few non-all-inclusive Marmári hotels, recently refurbished. Low-rise bungalows ring a large, wind-protected pool, with family quads in the rear wing. Medium-sized upstairs doubles have bathrooms with butler sinks, fridges, double beds, beige walls, bright furnishings, plus large balconies overlooking gardens and pool.

Fenareti € *Mastihári, tel: 22420 59002, or 6948 882644;* http://fenareti. kosweb.com. 1980s-style hillside hotel in the most relaxed coastal settlement, overlooking mid-beach; mosaic-floored studio-units in a peaceful garden environment, with kitchen corners and mosquito nets.

Grecotel Kos Imperial Thalasso €€€€ *Psalídi, tel: 22420 58000*, www. kosimperial.com. Well-designed luxury spread where electric carts deliver you and luggage through lush vegetation to remoter bungalows (standard rooms in the main wing). All units are pleasantly old-fashioned. One of three adult pools (salt-water) has a 'lazy river' and 'tropical waterfall'. The Grecotel beach is poor; you'll happily spend more time by a pool, surrounded by non-slip travertine paving – except during nightly pool-bar entertainment (think Beatles tribute groups). The food is good and varied, wait-staff well-trained. The Elixir Spa indeed has thalasso-baths and jets, but also a naturally lit fresh-water pool plus numerous ayurvedic treatments and massages.

Irina Beach €€ studios, €€€ suites, *2km (1.2 miles) east of shore junction, Tingáki, tel: 22420 69850*, www.irinabeachhotel.com. Various well-kept units, from studios to family apartments. Upstairs double suites have a sofa to sleep a third, closet space for three, beam ceilings, sea-views over lawns, bathrooms with rain shower and butler sink. The large, garden-set pool is ideal when the hotel beach is unusable; a better one (no facilities) lies 200m/yards east.

Michelangelo Resort & Spa €€€€ *Ágios Fokás, tel: 22420 45810*, www. michelangelo.gr. Common areas have 'wow' factor, though grounds (with token landscaping) are stark. The signature spa has all usual treatments and goodies but feels dark. Several categories of rooms in tiered hillside wings are airy, most with at least partial views across to Turkey's Knidos Peninsula. Two full-service restaurants provide enough variety over a long stay; half-board is a popular option. An infinity pool with swim-up bar is not clichéd in its setting, and long enough to do serious swimming; there's a patch of sand-and-shingle beach below.

Olympia Mare €€ *1km (0.6 miles) southwest of town, beach side of road, Kardámena, tel: 22420 91711*, www.olympiamare.com. There are posher, all-inclusive establishments nearby, but none with Olympia Mare's position: twenty steps across the lawn to the sea. 1980s-built apartments – the bathrooms show it, though living areas are updated. Sleep a family of four; most have water-view verandas.

Palazzo del Mare €€€€€ *Marmári, tel: 22420 42320*, www.palazzodel mare.gr. Impressive luxury resort, whose main pool extends 400m/yards towards the beach. Some units amongst eight accommodation types access semi-private, ultra-long pools. Plus points for courtesy afternoon day-rooms, prior to evening departures; minus ones for no in-room Wi-Fi, and no natural light in the gym/spa, the latter accessibly priced. The hotel is hard to find – leave the main highway at Limnára turning, then keep left at every junction.

NÍSYROS

Porfyris €€ *Mandráki centre, tel: 22420 31376*, www.porfyrishotel.gr. The most comfortable conventional hotel here, whose rooms got two makeovers since 2009, though breakfast still needs a rethink. Balconies overlook either Kámbos and the sea, hillside or the large ozone-purified pool.

Romantzo € *Mandráki port, tel: 22420 31340*, www.nisyros-romantzo.gr. The best budget choice on Nísyros, updated basalt-clad rooms and studios, not all with bay views – though there's a huge communal terrace on the top floor. Breakfast is surprisingly good. Minimal road noise; ample parking.

Ta Liotridia €€€ *shore lane near the windmill, Mandráki, tel: 22420 31580,* www.nisyros-taliotridia.com. Two suites in a restored olive mill – one of the few such projects here – for up to four people; worth the price for the terraces and volcanic-stone-and-wood decor. Lively bar downstairs.

KÁLYMNOS

Acroyiali € *Myrtiés, below lower road, tel: 22430 47521,* www.acroy ali.gr. Exceptionally tasteful, quiet sea-view apartments, with col-our splashes against marble flooring, each sleeping four; you're five steps from the best bit of Myrtiés beach. Advance booking mandatory.

Masouri Blu €€€ *bottom of steps down from main plaza, Masoúri, tel* 22430 47451, www.masouriblu.gr. 'Step into the Blue' is the motto of this friendly, new boutique hotel. Pastel-hued room furnishings and tiling in bathrooms, some with rain showers. Sea-side units have knockout views; some family rooms (kids nominal extra charge). Breakfast by the water; sunbeds on the best patch of local beach. Masouri Blu is popular with wedding parties, given its ample com-mon areas. Open into Nov provided there are advanced bookings.

Villa Melina €€ *Evangelístria district, Póthia, tel: 22430 22682,* www. villa-melina.com. Póthia's top choice: either rooms in a late 19th-century sponge magnate's mansion, or modern studios and family apartments around the fresh-water pool and gardens. The Garden-er's Studio Cottage at the back is charming. Good buffet breakfasts served on the patio; a warm welcome from owners Andonis and Themelina. Open all year.

TÉLENDOS

Porto Potha € *north edge of settlement, tel: 22430 47321,* www. telendoshotel.gr. This modern hotel offers 1980s-vintage standard doubles, large studios in a separate wing, and two new suites fitting four. There's a large pool, good patch of tamarisk-shaded beach and friendly managing family.

PSÉRIMOS

Psérimos Village €€€€ *Avlákia tel: 22430 59905,* www.hhotels.eu/pserimos-village. New, no-expense-spared cottage hotel: pure-stone walls, quality wood ceilings and floor-tiles. There are 18 cottages, ranging from single-space studios to open-plan galleried with loft double bed, sofa-beds downstairs, or double bedroom on a lower-ground floor, plus twins upstairs. Some houses take six, in two bedrooms plus on sofa-beds. All units have a bathroom, with shower alcoves. Family/group houses present full kitchens with proper stoves and huge fridges for serious cooking. All have shaded front patios, the best sea views from two upstairs studios. Pool planned for 2016, but the beach is only a few steps away; free sunbeds provided. Open all year.

LÉROS

Archontiko Angelou €€€ *signposted well inland, Álinda, tel: 22470 22749,* www.hotel-angelou-leros.com. Atmospheric converted 1895 mansion amidst orchards, akin to a French country hotel. Two of eight units (two are suites) have balconies; Victorian taps, beamed or decorated ceilings, old-tile (ground floor) or plank (upstairs) floors, antique furnishings throughout. A TV-free zone, and retro fans swish overhead, but downstairs rooms have mini-fridges. The upstairs lounge sports murals, while the garden-bar positions tables amongst shrubbery. Breakfast charged separately, gluten-free available. Open 1 Apr–15 Nov.

Crithoni's Paradise €€ rooms, €€€€ suites *Krithóni, inland, tel: 22470 25120,* www.crithonisparadisehotel.com. Léros's only mega-resort, a low-rise hillside complex of four wings with a smallish pool, disabled access and large, well-appointed rooms – though subject (like everywhere locally) to mosquito invasion. Decent buffet breakfast; affordable poolside drinks. Open all year.

Nefeli studios €€, apartments €€€ *Krithóni, tel: 22470 24611,* www.nefelihotels-leros.com. Amidst bougainvillea, lantana, rosemary, fig trees and patches of lawn stand these bungalow studios, apartments and suites, many with bay view. All units feature stone flooring and window surrounds, brightly painted wood trim and light-blue, white or turquoise soft furnishings (including good bedding). A quality breakfast features cake-of-the-day; the in-house bar has snacks besides drinks and good music. There's no pool, but beyond the big car-park is Krithóni cove itself, fine for a quick swim. Staff are helpful to a fault. Open all year; winter suite rental by the month.

Tony's Beach €€ *Vromólithos beach, tel: 22470 24742,* www.tonysbeach. com. Spacious two-room units, with big terraces looking to a small pool or the sea. Designer bathrooms have butler sinks, but kitchen corners are rudimentary – two hobs and a small fridge, so breakfast included. Disabled access and ample parking; free beach sunbeds.

PÁTMOS

Asteri €€ *Netiá district, Skála, tel: 22470 32465,* www.asteripatmos.gr. Secluded hilltop hotel with lovely gardens out front, sea-views west towards Ikaría, easy parking, a cozy lounge, and breakfasts featuring own-grown produce. Pay a bit extra for superior doubles offering more modern bathrooms and bigger balconies.

Blue Bay €€ *last building in town going east, Konsoláto district, Skála, tel: 22470 31165,* www.bluebaypatmos.gr. Blue Bay hasn't the midnight ferry and 4am fishing-boat noise that blights most Konsoláto hotels. Rooms, with blue furnishings and wood trim, also have fridges and balconies (most with bay-and-islet view), if basic bathrooms. Decent breakfasts and an appealing bar. Open Easter to early Nov.

Porto Scoutari rooms €€, suites €€€ *1km (0.6 miles) north of Skála, Melóï hillside, tel: 22470 33124* www.portoscoutari.com. Comfortable, three-wing hotel overlooking islets and the sunrise. Self-described as 'Romantic Hotel and Suites', thus geared to wedding parties or honeymooners – the pool is even heart-shaped. Constantly amidst rolling renovations; the best-value units are deluxe sea-view doubles in the middle wing. Excellent breakfasts; small spa/gym.

Studios Mathios € *Sápsila Cove, tel: 22470 32583,* www.mathiosapart ments.gr. With a vehicle, these bucolically set superior studios and apartment make an idyllic base, with their creative furnishing, extensive gardens and welcoming hosts Theologos and Giakoumina. The two adjacent coves, however, are not among Pátmos' best.

INDEX

INSIGHT ⊙ GUIDES POCKET GUIDE

KOS

First Edition 2016

Editor: Carine Tracanelli
Author: Marc Dubin
Head of Production: Rebeka Davies
Picture Editor: Tom Smyth
Cartography Update: Carte
Update Production: AM Services
Photography Credits: Alamy 5MC, 41, 59, 99;
Britta Jaschinski/Apa Publications 5TC, 6MC,
6TL, 6ML, 6ML, 7TC, 9R, 10, 13, 30, 33, 35, 39,
60, 62, 65, 92, 96, 100, 102; Corbis 5BL, 9, 23,
87; Getty Images 4MC, 4ML, 7M, 14, 18, 24,
28, 48, 84, 89, 90, 94, 104; iStock 4TC, 4TL, 5T,
5M, 5MC, 7M, 8R, 36, 46, 51, 54, 56, 70, 78, 83,
91; Mark Dubin 7T, 8L, 21, 43, 52, 66, 68, 72,
74, 76; Shutterstock 6TL, 44
Cover Pictures: front: iStock;
back: Shutterstock

Distribution
UK, Ireland and Europe: Apa Publications
(UK) Ltd; sales@insightguides.com
United States and Canada: Ingram Publisher
Services; ips@ingramcontent.com
Australia and New Zealand: Woodslane;
info@woodslane.com.au
Southeast Asia: Apa Publications (SN) Pte;
singaporeoffice@insightguides.com
Hong Kong, Taiwan and China:
Apa Publications (HK) Ltd;
hongkongoffice@insightguides.com

Worldwide: Apa Publications (UK) Ltd;
sales@insightguides.com

**Special Sales, Content Licensing
and CoPublishing**
Insight Guides can be purchased in bulk
quantities at discounted prices. We can create
special editions, personalised jackets and
corporate imprints tailored to your needs.
sales@insightguides.com;
www.insightguides.biz

Contact us
Every effort has been made to provide
accurate information in this publication,
but changes are inevitable. The publisher
cannot be responsible for any resulting loss,
inconvenience or injury. We would appreciate
it if readers would call our attention to any
errors or outdated information. We also
welcome your suggestions; please contact us
at: hello@insightguides.com
www.insightguides.com